T0090731

Cambridge Elements ☰

Elements on Women in the History of Philosophy
edited by
Jacqueline Broad
Monash University

MARY WOLLSTONECRAFT

Martina Reuter
University of Jyväskylä

CAMBRIDGE
UNIVERSITY PRESS

Shaftesbury Road, Cambridge CB2 8EA, United Kingdom

One Liberty Plaza, 20th Floor, New York, NY 10006, USA

477 Williamstown Road, Port Melbourne, VIC 3207, Australia

314–321, 3rd Floor, Plot 3, Splendor Forum, Jasola District Centre,
New Delhi – 110025, India

103 Penang Road, #05–06/07, Visioncrest Commercial, Singapore 238467

Cambridge University Press is part of Cambridge University Press & Assessment,
a department of the University of Cambridge.

We share the University's mission to contribute to society through the pursuit of
education, learning and research at the highest international levels of excellence.

www.cambridge.org
Information on this title: www.cambridge.org/9781009010610

DOI: 10.1017/9781009023924

© Martina Reuter 2022

This publication is in copyright. Subject to statutory exception and to the provisions
of relevant collective licensing agreements, no reproduction of any part may take
place without the written permission of Cambridge University Press & Assessment.

First published 2022

A catalogue record for this publication is available from the British Library.

ISBN 978-1-009-01061-0 Paperback
ISSN 2634-4645 (online)
ISSN 2634-4637 (print)

Cambridge University Press & Assessment has no responsibility for the persistence
or accuracy of URLs for external or third-party internet websites referred to in this
publication and does not guarantee that any content on such websites is, or will
remain, accurate or appropriate.

Mary Wollstonecraft

Elements on Women in the History of Philosophy

DOI: 10.1017/9781009023924
First published online: September 2022

Martina Reuter
University of Jyväskylä

Author for correspondence: Martina Reuter, anna.m.reuter@jyu.fi

Abstract: Mary Wollstonecraft is recognized as an important early feminist. This Element argues that she is also an ingenious moral philosopher, who showed that true virtue and the liberty of women are necessarily interdependent. The Element consists of eight sections. After an introduction, Section 2 discusses Wollstonecraft's concept of reason by examining its metaphysical foundation and its role as moral capacity. According to Wollstonecraft, reason interacts closely with the passions. Then, Sections 3 and 4 discuss the roles of the passions and the imagination. Reason, passion and imagination all come together in Wollstonecraft's discussions of love and friendship, which are the topic of Section 5. Wollstonecraft values education and knowledge, but discussions of her epistemology have been rare. Section 6 analyses some aspects of her views on knowledge. Finally, Section 7 discusses Wollstonecraft's notion of virtue, including its relations to liberty and duty. Section 8 draws some general conclusions.

Keywords: Mary Wollstonecraft, virtue, reason, passion, imagination

© Martina Reuter 2022

ISBNs: 9781009010610 (PB), 9781009023924 (OC)
ISSNs: 2634-4645 (online), 2634-4637 (print)

Contents

1 Introduction

At one point in *A Vindication of the Rights of Woman* (1792), Mary Wollstonecraft positions herself as a philosopher and moralist. She writes: 'As a philosopher, I read with indignation the plausible epithets which men use to soften their insults; and as a moralist, I ask what is meant by such heterogeneous associations, as fair defects, amiable weaknesses, &c.?' (*Works* 5: 103). Most often the 'sagacious' or 'short-sighted philosopher' is a target of Wollstonecraft's criticism (*Works* 5: 13, 57). Moralists are similarly limited in their thinking, most often because they hold prejudiced opinions on women (e.g. *Works* 5: 130). By identifying herself as a philosopher and as a moralist, Wollstonecraft underlines that the problem is the misuse of these disciplines, not the disciplines themselves. In order to approach her as a moral philosopher, we need to begin here.

When positively defined, a philosopher is someone in search for truth and a moralist is a defender of the true principles of morality, which depend on perfection and strength, not on defect and weakness. Wollstonecraft is a passionate lover of truth. She presents a broad concept of reason (discussed in Section 2), but favours reason understood as an ability to perceive and even to desire truth. It is no coincidence that when Wollstonecraft speaks approvingly of 'a great philosopher', she is referring to Plato, known for his account of intuitive – as opposed to deductive – knowledge (*Works* 5: 23; also Tomaselli 2019). In *A Vindication of the Rights of Men* (1790), she mentions Plato and John Milton as sources of the idea that earthly love can lead to heavenly love and is ultimately a love of perfection (*Works* 5: 46). Wollstonecraft's Plato was inspired by the Christianized Plato of Milton's poetry and by Richard Price's writings.[1]

Richard Price is one of three interlocutors who will frame my interpretation of Wollstonecraft's moral philosophy. The two others are Jean-Jacques Rousseau and Catharine Macaulay. Price was the only one Wollstonecraft knew in person,

---

[1] We do not know if Wollstonecraft read any of Plato's dialogues. She makes no direct references to his works or to having read any of them. It has been claimed that there were no English translations of Plato's works available to her (Bergès and Coffee 2016: 7), but as pointed out by Karen Green (2019: 231), this is not the case. Wollstonecraft would have had access to, for example, *Phedon: or, a Dialogue of the Immortality of the Soul. From Plato the Divine Philosopher* (Plato 1777) and *The Banquet, a Dialogue of Plato Concerning Love* (Plato 1767; the title page bears the addition 'The Second Part', but the volume includes Plato's *Symposium* as a whole). Instead of focusing on translations available when Wollstonecraft embarked on her writing career, some scholars examining Wollstonecraft's Platonism have concentrated on her possible acquaintance during her youth with Thomas Taylor, who published an English translation of Plato's *Phaedrus* in 1792 (Todd 2000: 27, 461n13; Tomaselli 2019). I find it more likely that Wollstonecraft may have read published translations of Plato's dialogues, in particular those focusing on the topics of beauty, love and immortality, than that she would have had access to Taylor's unpublished translation when she wrote *Rights of Men* and *Rights of Woman*. By the early 1790s, Taylor was an opponent of the cause for the rights of women, which he ridiculed in his anonymously published *Vindication of the Rights of Brutes* (1792); see Todd (2000: 185, 474n21).

but all three thinkers are solid interlocutors in the sense that Wollstonecraft discusses their works in some detail. Wollstonecraft wrote her first explicitly philosophical work, *A Vindication of the Rights of Men*, as a criticism of Edmund Burke's attack on Price's defence of the French Revolution. Rousseau, on the other hand, is by far Wollstonecraft's most famous interlocutor. She engaged in a critical dialogue with his works that lasted throughout her intellectual career and included praise of his genius (*Letters*: 114–15) as well as severe criticism of his views on the moral education of women (e.g. *Works* 5: 108–12). Finally, Macaulay, who was one of the most famous intellectual women of her time, influenced Wollstonecraft as both a role model and philosophical source. We do not know to what extent Wollstonecraft was familiar with Macaulay's works before she read the latter's *Letters on Education* (1790), but Wollstonecraft's long review of it is one of her most systematic discussions of several essential philosophical questions, including the problem of free will (*Works* 7: 309–22). It is also evident that Macaulay's critical remarks on Rousseau's account of gendered virtue had a profound impact on the detailed criticism Wollstonecraft develops in *Rights of Woman*, published less than two years after the review (see also Gunther-Canada 2003).

We know that these three authors influenced Wollstonecraft's philosophical thought, but my main aim is not to trace influences. I will rather refer to their works – and to those of several other thinkers – in order to sketch the philosophical context in which Wollstonecraft developed her thought. Sometimes my comparisons delve a bit deeper into positions she only hints at. Sometimes I refer to differences between authors in order to show the specificities of her thought. Wollstonecraft develops her most detailed discussions of moral philosophy in *Rights of Woman*. I use that book as my main source, complemented by her other writings when relevant.

When compared to many other women philosophers, Wollstonecraft has received a fair amount of scholarly attention. In addition to many biographies casting light on her eventful life (e.g. Todd 2000), monographs by Virginia Sapiro (1992), Wendy Gunther-Canada (2001), Barbara Taylor (2003), Natalie Fuehrer Taylor (2007), and Sylvana Tomaselli (2021) have developed detailed studies of Wollstonecraft's writings from the perspectives of political theory and intellectual history. In recent years, philosophers have focused increasingly on Wollstonecraft's concept of freedom defined as liberty from arbitrary power, such as the power of non-constitutional monarchs or the power of husbands over wives, who do not have full rights as legal persons. This interpretation, which places Wollstonecraft in the republican tradition of political thought, has been influentially defended by Lena Halldenius (2007, 2014, 2015, 2016), Alan Coffee (2013, 2014, 2016), and Sandrine Bergès (2013, 2016). Halldenius has traced Wollstonecraft's critical dialogue with the republican tradition in great detail and synthesized the feminist political philosophy which grows out of this dialogue (Halldenius 2015).

My interpretation of Wollstonecraft's moral philosophy is embedded in the republican reading, not least in the sense that the three main interlocutors I discuss – Price, Rousseau and Macaulay – are among Wollstonecraft's most important fellow republicans, but my focus is different. Rather than discussing her detailed analyses of arbitrary power or her concept of liberty and its political implications, I concentrate on her moral psychology and its metaphysical basis. Wollstonecraft's metaphysical views are intertwined with her theological views and I hope to show that by paying some attention to the latter, one finds philosophical consistency in her system of thought, which may on the surface appear unsystematic.

The Element consists of six thematic sections followed by a Conclusion. First, in Section 2 I set out Wollstonecraft's concept of reason by examining its metaphysical relations to Providence and liberty as well as its role as the most important mental capacity. According to Wollstonecraft's view, reason acts in close collaboration with the passions. In Section 3 I explore the various roles of the passions, and in Section 4, that of the imagination, the third of the mental capacities that constitute the basis for Wollstonecraft's moral psychology. Reason, passion and imagination all come together in Wollstonecraft's discussions of love and friendship, which I examine in Section 5. It is well known that Wollstonecraft values education and knowledge, but few scholars discuss her epistemology. In Section 6, I analyse some aspects of her views on knowledge, with a focus on elements of innateness and empiricist influences. Finally, in Section 7 I discuss Wollstonecraft's notion of virtue, including its unity and its relations to liberty and duty.

2 Reason

Wollstonecraft is well known for her strong emphasis on reason. At the very beginning of *Rights of Woman*, she lists 'the most simple truths' on which morality as well as society at large must be built. The first truth is posited as a question: 'In what does man's pre-eminence over the brute creation consist? The answer is as clear as that a half is less than the whole; in Reason' (*Works* 5: 81). Wollstonecraft's concept of reason is fundamental to her thought as a whole and refers to a metaphysical entity as well as a capacity of the human mind. In this section, I will first discuss the metaphysical aspects of reason by focusing in Subsection 2.1 on its relation with Providence and in Subsection 2.2 on its relation with liberty. Subsection 2.3 addresses reason as a mental capacity.

2.1 Reason and Providence

From a metaphysical point of view, reason is different from other human capacities because it is an immaterial entity, which is immutable and indestructible. 'The stamen of immortality', according to Wollstonecraft, 'is the perfectibility of human reason' (*Works* 5: 122). God posits perfect reason, and Wollstonecraft perceives reason as the most important of the divine attributes. She emphasizes that when submitting to God, she is submitting to 'unerring *reason*' and to 'the authority of reason' (*Works* 5: 34, 170). Like many Enlightenment thinkers, Wollstonecraft emphasizes that humans must submit only to reason. In her case, reason is simultaneously an external authority, deriving its power from God, and an internal authority, imprinted on the human mind.

Humans differ in how well they use their reason, but the capacity belongs equally to all. Wollstonecraft writes:

> More or less may be conspicuous in one being than another; but the nature of reason must be the same in all, if it be an emanation of divinity, the tie that connects the creature with the Creator; for, can that soul be stamped with the heavenly image, that is not perfected by the exercise of its own reason?
>
> (*Works* 5: 122)

Reason connects all human beings with each other and with their Creator, and distinguishes humans from those parts of creation that are made solely of matter. Non-rational creatures are governed by mechanical laws, but due to their rational natures, humans are self-governing: '[A]n immortal soul, not restrained by mechanical laws and struggling to free itself from the shackles of matter, contributes to, instead of disturbing, the order of creation, when, co-operating with the Father of spirits, it tries to govern itself by the invariable rule that . . . regulates the universe' (*Works* 5: 116).

Wollstonecraft's view of how self-governing humans contribute to the order of creation is an important aspect of her understanding of human agency and its relation to Providence. She occasionally mentions Providence, but does not discuss it in detail. We can better understand the metaphysical basis for her view if we compare it with Richard Price's essay 'On Providence', in his *Four Dissertations* (1767), a work that Wollstonecraft recommended to her friend George Blood in January 1788 (*Letters*: 147).[2]

Price criticizes the idea of Providence as a pre-established order and defends an understanding that God produces Providence 'by constant influences, rather than such an original establishment' (Price 1767: 64). Divine agency is the first, but not the immediate cause of every particular event (Price 1767: 52). In the

---

[2] For a discussion of Price's and Wollstonecraft's theological views, see Reuter (2010: 108–13).

material world, Providence is administered in accordance with the laws of nature. Price makes frequent references to Isaac Newton and to works on the compatibility between Newton's theory and Christianity (e.g., Price 1767: 53). He holds that the Deity 'is properly the *life* of [the creation], the *infinite Spirit* by which it is informed and sustained; that all material causes are no more than instruments in his hand, and that from him their efficiency is derived' (Price 1767: 54). Price emphasizes that the 'first mover cannot be matter itself' (Price 1767: 51). His account is explicitly Platonist and he refers to Plato's *Laws* 10 (898 c, 900 c–d, 902 d–e) when arguing that '*mind* must be *prior* to *matter*, and the cause of all its modifications and changes; and that, therefore, there is an universal mind possest of all perfection, which produced and which actuates all things' (Price 1767: 10).

Rational human beings are also instruments of Providence, but in a significantly different way to that of mere material beings. According to Price, the 'doctrine of Providence … ought never to be explained in such a manner as to destroy the value of the agency of created beings' (Price 1767: 94). The Deity has taken care 'to give his reasonable creatures room for a proper exertion of their faculties, and for the practice of virtue' (Price 1767: 66–7). Price is not as bold as Wollstonecraft. He does not claim that reasonable creatures co-operate with their Creator, but he formulates an understanding of Providence that leaves room for Wollstonecraft's interpretation. God is the first cause of everything that happens, but human agents are immediate causes and since they are spiritual beings, they can be causes in a truer sense than mere matter.[3] Thus humans can, in Wollstonecraft's words, contribute to the order of creation.

2.2 Reason and Liberty

Reason is closely related to liberty. Price notes that human beings, whom he categorizes as 'the lowest order of reasonable Beings', abuse their liberty time and again, but it would be 'absurd to ask why was liberty granted them' (Price 1767: 118–19).[4] He emphasizes that liberty is 'essential to intelligence, and to all rational and moral happiness' (Price 1767: 119). Without liberty, reasonable beings would 'not exist at all' (Price 1767: 119). This is so because reasoning

---

[3] Price and Wollstonecraft are dualists in the sense that they separate spirit and matter, and believe in the afterlife of the soul as a distinct entity. Sylvana Tomaselli has recently claimed that Wollstonecraft 'believed in the existence of two substances, a physical and an immaterial one' (2021: 100). It is important to note, though, that Wollstonecraft's dualism resembles Plato's rather than Descartes'. She holds that spirit infuses matter and she shares Price's Platonist idea of spirit as activity. On Price's dualism, see Hickman (2019).

[4] On Price's view of liberty and necessity, see also Harris (2005: 135–7); and Greenberg (2013: 259–60).

beings, as we saw in the previous subsection (Subsection 2.1), are immediate causes of their own actions. In this context, liberty is indistinguishable from the ability to act as a self-governing cause. Reasoning human beings may, as Price emphasizes, abuse their liberty and fall into error, but they may also improve themselves and reach truths.

As Wollstonecraft understands it, the possibility of error is a crucial aspect of human reasoning. Making errors distinguishes humans from God, who possesses perfect reason, as well as from non-human animals, which possess neither reason nor liberty. Animals act automatically on the basis of their God-given instincts, without deliberation. This means that they neither err nor improve themselves. In her didactic children's book *Original Stories from Real Life* (1788), Wollstonecraft discusses the behaviour of birds and points out that 'the first nest they make and the last are exactly the same' (*Works* 4: 372). Birds do not make errors. They have an instinctive ability to build appropriate nests, but since they lack reason and imagination, they cannot improve their ability.[5] Humans, however, have reason, which is 'the simple power of improvement; or, more properly speaking, of discerning truth' (*Works* 5: 122). This power needs to be strengthened through exercise, and these exercises may often include making errors. At one point Wollstonecraft concedes that 'erroneous opinions [are] better than none at all' (*Works* 5: 257). She points out that under prevailing social circumstances:

> It should seem, that one reason why men have superior judgment, and more fortitude than women, is undoubtedly this, that they give a freer scope to the grand passions, and by more frequently going astray enlarge their minds. If then by the exercise of their own reason they fix on some stable principle, they have probably to thank the force of their passions, nourished by *false* views of life. (*Works* 5: 179)

I will discuss the manifold philosophical roles Wollstonecraft gives the passions in the next section (Section 3), but here they may cause error and have to be contested by reason. The same meaning is found right at the beginning of *Rights of Woman*, where Wollstonecraft writes that by struggling with the passions, humans 'attain a degree of knowledge denied to the brutes' (*Works* 5: 81). Animals have neither reason nor human passions. They do not fall into error, but neither do they attain knowledge.

---

[5] Like most of her contemporaries, Wollstonecraft thought that animals belonged to a lower order of creation than humans, but this did not allow for disrespect and even less for cruelty: quite the contrary. In *Original Stories*, Wollstonecraft teaches the importance of treating animals well (*Works* 4: 367–87). Since humans are higher creatures, they have a responsibility for animals. Wollstonecraft discusses the cognitive capacities of animals in her review of William Smellie's *Philosophy of Natural History* (1790) (*Works* 7: 295–300). On Wollstonecraft's views in the context of her time, see Spencer (2012), and for a discussion of her views on animal ethics, see Botting (2016).

Reasoning is the key to improvement and to human liberty. The relation between reason and liberty is twofold: deliberation requires liberty, and reasoning produces independence. According to Wollstonecraft, it 'is the right use of reason alone which makes us independent of every thing – excepting the unclouded Reason' (*Works* 5: 190). Like Price, she holds that humans are free beings because they reason, not as such because they possess a free will. She did not deny the existence of free will, but she rarely mentions the will as a separate mental capacity.

In *A Vindication of the Rights of Woman*, Wollstonecraft refers to the will in order to emphasize the non-voluntary nature of an instantaneous association of ideas, which 'seems rather to depend on the original temperature of the mind than on the will' (*Works* 5: 185). In another passage, she refers to 'a free-will offering to Him' in order to emphasize the voluntary nature that is characteristic of a true love of God (*Works* 5: 232). The opposition between reason and mere will is explicated in a passage where Wollstonecraft criticizes the habit of teaching girls 'slavishly to submit to their parents': if parents 'insist on their children submitting to their will merely because it is their will', these children will never achieve 'rational freedom' (*Works* 5: 227). Humans have a free will, but true freedom is achieved only when one acts in accordance with reason.

Wollstonecraft develops her most detailed discussion of the will in a review of Catharine Macaulay's *Letters on Education: with Observations on Religious and Metaphysical Subjects* (1790). Macaulay defends a position she calls 'moral necessity' against that of 'free-willers' (Macaulay 1996: 454–507). Like Price and Wollstonecraft, she grounds her position in theology, with consequences for human moral psychology. Macaulay defends a form of intellectualism according to which God created the world to eternal standards. In her view, since God is guided by perfect reason, God *necessarily* chooses the best possible principles. She writes that 'subjection to this necessity, is the peculiar glory of the divine character' (Macaulay 1996: 462). Human beings are imperfect, but in a similar fashion necessitated by truth. Macaulay holds that 'the nearer approaches which all finite creatures make to the perfections of their creator, the more they will be brought under the blessed subjection of being necessarily determined in their volitions by right principles of conduct' (Macaulay 1996: 462).[6] Macaulay's free-willers, on the other hand, are voluntarists, who argue that God created the world and its principles by an act of free

---

[6] Macaulay develops her position at greater length in her earlier work *A Treatise on the Immutability of Moral Truth* (Macaulay Graham 1783). On her position, see also Reuter (2007: 150–4); O'Brien (2009: 165–8); and Green (2020: 152–63).

will (Macaulay 1996: 458–9). The position goes hand in hand with an emphasis on the human will, which must be undetermined in order to be free.

Price and Wollstonecraft also hold intellectualist views of creation but, as ably argued by Karen O'Brien, 'they stopped short of the "philosophical necessity" espoused by Macaulay and Priestley' (O'Brien 2009: 187). With David Hartley, Joseph Priestley defended an explicitly necessitarian view that human will is always necessitated by motives (Greenberg 2013: 248).[7] In her laudatory review of *Letters on Education*, Wollstonecraft mildly reproaches Macaulay for simplifying the position of the free-willers.[8] She points out that few defenders of free will claim that the will 'can choose either good or evil, without being influenced by any motive' (*Works* 7: 320). Actually, Wollstonecraft writes, the 'virtuous Free-Willer still continues to cultivate his mind with as much care, that he may discern good from evil, and choose accordingly' (*Works* 7: 321). Wollstonecraft defends free-willers against charges of arbitrariness and points out that defenders of moral necessity and defenders of free will actually act in more or less the same way in order to achieve virtue. Both camps agree that in order to act virtuously, humans must act in accordance with reason. In her review, Wollstonecraft leaves open the ultimate metaphysical question of whether motives determine the will or whether the will chooses freely between different influencing motives. She claims that the ultimate relation between the understanding and the will is 'a question, which metaphysicians have not yet brought to an issue' (*Works* 7: 321).

Wollstonecraft pinpoints what Sean Greenberg has characterized as 'a standoff' between eighteenth-century libertarians and necessitarians. Both sides intend to promote virtue and piety, but to do so, they rely on opposite metaphysical positions (Greenberg 2013: 262). Wollstonecraft does not take a stand on the controversy between libertarians, who claim that the will must under all circumstances be uncaused in order to be free, and necessitarians like Macaulay, who claim that humans are most free when their volitions are 'necessarily determined' by the understanding (Macaulay 1996: 462). Wollstonecraft emphasizes that the will is always acting upon some motive and that motives must be based on reason if one is to act virtuously. She holds that motives must be chosen freely in the sense that they are not determined by either God or mechanical laws. Humans are self-governing immediate causes of their actions, but Wollstonecraft gives no clear answer as to whether she thinks that the fully

---

[7] According to Sean Greenberg, 'Hartley's work was one of the chief, though unstated, targets of Price's writings on freedom'. Priestley, on the other hand, 'defended necessitarianism in a celebrated, amicable exchange of letters with Price' (Greenberg 2013: 249).

[8] For further discussions of Wollstonecraft's review of Macaulay's *Letters on Education*, see Reuter (2007); O'Brien (2009: 176); and Tomaselli (2021: 103–4).

developed understanding determines the will to act virtuously or that the will is still at that point free to act against the motives presented by the understanding. She seems to find it irrelevant whether the human ability to govern oneself is ultimately based on the understanding or the will. The important question concerns the human ability to develop one's understanding by the free use of reason.

Rather than trying to pinpoint the exact metaphysical relation between reason and liberty, Wollstonecraft emphasizes that the two are necessarily related and that this necessary relation has moral and political consequences. She shares this emphasis with Price. In *A Discourse on the Love of Our Country*, Price reminds us that 'Liberty is … inseparable from knowledge and virtue' (Price 1991: 184). Here liberty is understood in its political meaning and Price draws the conclusion that an 'enlightened and virtuous country must be a free country' (Price 1991: 184).[9] In the opening passage of *A Vindication of the Rights of Men*, defending Price against Burke's attack, Wollstonecraft explains that she contends 'for the *rights of men* and the liberty of reason' (*Works* 5: 7). In *A Vindication of the Rights of Woman* she explicitly extends the demand to woman and writes that 'as sound politics diffuse liberty, mankind, including woman, will become more wise and virtuous' (*Works* 5: 106). The metaphysical idea of self-governing humans serves as the basis for a right and a duty to be morally and politically self-governing.[10] To put it the other way round, in order to make the desired moral and political demands, one needs to hold that humans are able to govern themselves, but one does not need to take a final metaphysical stand on whether humans ultimately govern themselves due to their will or their reason. Therefore Price, Priestley, Macaulay and Wollstonecraft are quite able to share the same political demands despite differences in metaphysical detail.

2.3 The Exercises of Reason

We have seen that reason needs to be exercised so that humans can achieve truth and become independent beings, but what exactly does Wollstonecraft mean by the exercise of reason? When Wollstonecraft refers to reason as a human mental capacity, she writes about 'discerning truth' (*Works* 5: 122), about 'the power of generalizing ideas' (*Works* 5: 123), and she describes how 'reason deduces' (*Works* 5: 34). It is important to note that when perceived as a human capacity, reason may itself be defective. Wollstonecraft refers to 'that sluggish reason, which supinely takes opinion on trust and obstinately supports them to spare

---

[9] On the relations between Price's theological metaphysics and his radical political opinions, see Hickman (2019); also Hutton (2021: 191).

[10] On Wollstonecraft's understanding of the relations between rights and duties, see Halldenius (2007; 2015: 33–49).

itself the labour of thinking' (*Works* 5: 264). Reasoning and 'the cultivation of the understanding' (*Works* 5: 123) are closely related, but not always synonyms. When Wollstonecraft refers to the understanding, she is sometimes referring to a capacity and sometimes to the outcome of exercising one's faculties. In the latter case, the understanding becomes affiliated with knowledge. In Subsection 2.2, we saw that the refinement of judgement depends on the passions. A similar interaction between different capacities of the mind holds for the cultivation of the understanding (also Tomaselli 2021: 96).

Wollstonecraft refers to the capacity for deduction when she discusses the deduction of laws and rules. In *Rights of Woman*, she emphasizes that one cannot 'educate moral beings by any other rules than those deduced from pure reason' (*Works* 5: 101). This formulation brings to mind Immanuel Kant's deduction of the categorical imperative, but there are two important differences between Wollstonecraft's and Kant's views. First, whereas Kant's pure reason is purely formal and void of substantial content, Wollstonecraft's pure reason is pure in the sense of being unaffected by non-rational desires or, she would add, relations of dependence that affect the independence of reason. Her pure reason is substantial in the sense that it can discern truths – for example the truth of real good – from which it can deduce rules.[11] Second, whereas Kant and Wollstonecraft agree that reason is a standard internal to the human mind, for her it is also an external divine standard. In its purest form, her pure reason is the reason of God. This becomes clear from a passage in *Rights of Men*. Wollstonecraft points out that when submitting to God, 'it is not to an arbitrary will, but to unerring *reason* I submit' (*Works* 5: 34). She argues that from the conception of God as Creator and supreme unerring reason it follows that humans must submit to the moral laws they deduce from their dependence on him. The moral law is deduced from ultimate divine pure reason, upon which human reason is dependent. As J. B. Schneewind has argued regarding Price's similar position, the moral agent's dependence on an established moral law constitutes the main difference between Price's – and Wollstonecraft's – conception of self-governing and Kant's concept of autonomy, which rests on the idea of self-legislation, independent of any external foundation (Schneewind 1998: 514).[12]

As we have seen, Wollstonecraft occasionally refers to general laws and rules, but more often she writes about principles. To 'act from principle' is mostly presented in an approving light (e.g., *Works* 5: 176), but not all principles are good. A woman may be 'restrained by principle or prejudice' (*Works* 5: 96), the blind duty to obey a vicious being is 'the most arbitrary principle' (*Works* 5:

---

[11] I discuss the capacity to discern truth at the end of this Subsection.

[12] For a further discussion of Wollstonecraft's relation to Kantian philosophy and of how Schneewind's exclusion of Wollstonecraft affects his study of the invention of autonomy, see Reuter (2018).

224) and we may find 'antagonist principles' (*Works* 5: 46), which cannot be reconciled. Most valuable are the 'simple principles', which constitute a form of simple truths. At the beginning of *Rights of Woman*, in her dedicatory letter to the French revolutionary Charles Maurice de Talleyrand-Périgord, Wollstonecraft identifies two simple principles: that independence is 'the basis of every virtue' (*Works* 5: 65) and that 'truth must be common to all' (*Works* 5: 66). These principles are then characterized as 'immutable' (*Works* 5: 67). Wollstonecraft returns to the same simple and immutable principles of liberty and reason in her conclusions, where she claims to have opened 'a few simple principles' and cleared 'away the rubbish which obscured them' (*Works* 5: 254).

Simple principles are, according to Wollstonecraft, known, but principles can also be 'formed' or 'fixed upon' (e.g., *Works* 5: 117, 179). It is quite clear from her writings that the formation of principles requires more than mere deduction. In Subsection 2.2, we saw that men have, under present social conditions, superior judgement because they are allowed to give a freer scope to the passions: 'If then by the exercise of their own reason they fix on some stable principle, they have probably to thank the force of their passions' (*Works* 5: 179). Deduction is an activity internal to reason. Wollstonecraft's emphasis on the passions shows why deduction alone is not enough and why 'the deductions of reason' may even, as she claims in her *Hints*, 'destroy sublimity' (*Works* 5: 274). Simple and immutable principles are known by reason, but reason is, for Wollstonecraft, more than the capacity for deduction. Reason is also active when one is generalizing ideas and discerning truth. Both activities are essential to Wollstonecraft's epistemology. In Subsection 6.2, I will examine them and the tensions between the empiricist language of generalizing ideas and the rationalist language of discerning truth. Here, I want to conclude the discussion of reason by briefly comparing Wollstonecraft's remarks on how reason discerns truth and enables humans 'to discern good from evil' (*Works* 5: 14) with Price's similar views.

In *A Review of the Principal Questions and Difficulties in Morals* (1758), Price defines reason as 'the power within us that *understands*; the *Intuition* of the mind, or the faculty in it that discerns *truth*, that views, compares, and *judges* of all ideas and things; is a spring of new ideas' (Price 1758: 19–20). In a long footnote he explicitly distinguishes 'the two acts of the understanding ... intuition and deduction', and emphasizes that his primary interest is in intuition (Price 1758: 20). Price's main aim is to argue that moral ideas belong to reason, not to a distinct moral sense (see Subsection 4.1). His discussion is explicitly Platonist, and particularly refers to the dialogue *Theaetetus* (Price 1758: 52–3). Price's distinction between intuitive and deductive reason illuminates Wollstonecraft's distinction between reason as the capacity to discern truth, including moral truth, and reason as the capacity to deduce rules from these truths. The comparison with Price helps us grasp what can be characterized as Platonist elements in her thought. Still, when Wollstonecraft compares deduction and intuition in her *Hints*, she is connecting intuition with 'flights of imagination' and 'inspiration', not with reason (*Works* 5: 274). In this respect she differs from Price, according to whom imagination is a passive 'faculty nearly allied to *sense*' (Price 1758: 26). Wollstonecraft understands imagination and reason as close allies, not least because they are both capacities that humans have, but not other animals (*Works* 4: 372; *Letters*: 264). She shares with Price an understanding of intuited truth, attributable to Platonist influences, but hers is in many respects a more poetic Plato, inherited from Milton's poetry (*Works* 5: 46). In her view reason interacts closely with passion and imagination.

3 Passion

Wollstonecraft's interest in the passions was very much a feature of her times. As James A. Harris aptly puts it, it is 'no exaggeration to say that writers in eighteenth-century Britain were obsessed with the passions and their government' (Harris 2013: 270). This obsession was shared by those who, like Wollstonecraft and Price, grounded morality in reason with those who, like David Hume, grounded it in sentiments derived from the passions. The eighteenth-century interest was inherited from the previous century, but eighteenth-century authors were less interested than their predecessors in composing taxonomies of the passions. The vocabulary underwent changes and the terms 'passion' (from the Greek *pathos*) and 'affection' were accompanied by 'sentiment', 'feeling', 'emotion' and 'appetite' (Schmitter 2013).

Wollstonecraft's writings are typical examples of these changing trends. With the exception of love, she rarely discusses individual passions and she makes no attempt to compose a taxonomy of their respective characteristics. She uses all the terms listed above and her usage both reflects and occasionally modifies that of her contemporaries. She continuously uses 'passion' as her major term, not least when she discusses its relations with reason. As we will see, she sometimes uses other terms in order to describe something distinct from passion or some aspect of passion. Like her contemporaries, Wollstonecraft was obsessed with the particular question of how humans can govern the passions. Some early feminist interpreters of Wollstonecraft's thought were worried by what they saw as her overvaluing of masculine reason and undervaluing of passion, but recent interpreters tend to agree that in the context of her views as a whole and her times, she sees the passions as much more than an obstacle.[13] In this section, I will first discuss the role of the passions as necessary auxiliaries of reason. Subsection 3.1.1 focuses on the theological aspect of this question and Subsection 3.1.2 on the passions in moral psychology. In Subsection 3.2, I discuss the roles played by particular kinds of passions, emotions and feelings.

3.1 Passions as Necessary Auxiliaries

Wollstonecraft describes the passions as 'necessary auxiliaries of reason' (*Works* 5: 16) and we must begin by noting that the passions are necessary in two different respects. First, the passions constitute a necessary aspect of Wollstonecraft's (and Price's) understanding of Providence. Humans have to freely choose knowledge and virtue, and as we saw in Subsection 2.2, the passions often present obstacles to this choice in the form of false views. Second, the passions constitute a necessary part of Wollstonecraft's moral psychology. The two roles of the passions do often appear to be intertwined in Wollstonecraft's writings. Still, the distinction is important, because the two roles answer two separate questions. The connection to Providence answers the question of *why* humans have passions; the connection to moral psychology answers the question of *how* the passions affect human life and human capacities.

3.1.1 Passions and Providence

Wollstonecraft addresses the *why* question right at the beginning of *Rights of Woman* by asking: 'For what purpose were the passions implanted? That man by struggling with them might attain a degree of knowledge denied to the brutes' (*Works* 5: 81). We can distinguish at least two theological reasons why the passions are necessary: one related to the very nature of immortality and the other to the origin of evil.[14] Wollstonecraft holds that 'the perfectibility of human reason' is the 'stamen of immortality' (*Works* 5: 122). Not merely reason as such is immortal, but rather the act of reasoning. This statement is related to the idea of reason as a genuine cause participating in Providence, discussed in Subsection 2.1. Wollstonecraft continues that 'were man created perfect, or did a flood of knowledge break in upon him, when he arrived at maturity, that

---

[13] For an expression of this feminist worry, see Gatens (1991), and for early feminist interpretations acknowledging the role of the passions, see Sapiro (1992); Mackenzie (1993); Green (1997); Khin Zaw (1998). I discuss different feminist interpretations of Wollstonecraft's understanding of the passions in Reuter (2016: 51–4).

[14] In a recent discussion of Wollstonecraft's religious views, Sarah Hutton claims that in *Rights of Woman* Wollstonecraft was not concerned with absolving God from responsibility for evil (Hutton 2021: 191), but this seems to be a misinterpretation.

precluded error, I should doubt whether his existence would be continued after the dissolution of the body' (*Works* 5: 122). God is the only perfect immortal being. Humans are not created perfect, but perfectible. We need to use our reason and struggle with our passions to secure the immortality of our souls.

When Wollstonecraft is discussing the relation between the passions and evil, she provides an interesting critique of what she takes to be Rousseau's position on Providence. Right at the beginning of *Emile or On Education* (1762), Rousseau points out that 'Everything is good as it leaves the hands of the Author of things; everything degenerates in the hands of man' (Rousseau 1979: 37). Wollstonecraft attacks Rousseau for considering 'evil as positive'. She argues that his 'paradoxical exclamation, that God had made all things right, and that error has been introduced by the creature, whom he formed, knowing what he formed, is as unphilosophical as impious' (*Works* 5: 83). It is, in other words, a paradox to claim that God's creation is entirely good and, at the same time, that evil is introduced by one part of that creation, that is, the human being. Wollstonecraft claims that though the passions may cause evil, they are not in themselves a positive evil and they do not operate irrespectively of God's intentions. On the contrary, 'the passions should unfold our reason, because [God] could see that present evil would produce future good' (*Works* 5: 83).

Wollstonecraft's criticism of what she claims to be Rousseau's positive concept of evil is part of her criticism of what she saw as his idealized picture of the state of nature. She contrasts his claimed yearning for this state with her own conception of the perfectibility of human nature, and in particular of human reason.[15] Wollstonecraft agrees with Rousseau that 'misery and disorder [pervade in] society' (*Works* 5: 83), but disagrees on the remedy. She writes:

> [H]ad Rousseau mounted one step higher in his investigation, or could his eye have pierced through the foggy atmosphere, which he almost disdained to breathe, his active mind would have darted forward to contemplate the perfection of man in the establishment of true civilization, instead of taking his ferocious flight back to the night of sensual ignorance. (*Works* 5: 87)

Wollstonecraft's critique is not completely fair. Rousseau did not yearn for the ignorance of the state of nature, and his views on how one must moderate the passions in order to avoid evil and achieve good in many respects resemble those of Wollstonecraft. Still, her interpretation of where they differ on the providential role of the passions illuminates differences in their respective moral psychologies, which I will discuss next. Concerning Providence, we can conclude that Wollstonecraft's discussion of the providential basis of the

---

[15] On the differences between Rousseau's and Wollstonecraft's views on perfectibility, see Reuter (2014, 2017).

passions is important for two reasons. First, it shows her commitment to philosophical and theological consistency and second, it shows that though, in her opinion, the passions often cause error and even temporary evil, they are in themselves not only necessary but also inherently good, since they are part of God's creation.

3.1.2 Moral Psychology

Once Wollstonecraft has claimed that the passions are necessary auxiliaries of reason, she describes how they exercise the human capacity for thinking. She writes:

> a present impulse pushes us forward, and when we discover that the game did not deserve the chase, we find that we have gone over much ground, and not only gained many new ideas, but a habit of thinking. The exercise of our faculties is the great end, though not the goal we had in view when we started with such eagerness. (*Works* 5: 16)

Like where Wollstonecraft describes how the 'grand passions' exercise the use of reason (*Works* 5: 179, cited in Subsection 2.2), she is arguing here that chasing goals that may prove unworthy is still worthwhile, because the chase exercises the capacity for thinking. Rousseau holds a similar view on how passions and impressions prompt reasoning. In *Discourse on the Origin and Foundations of Inequality Among Mankind* (1755), he discusses the historical development of human mental capacities in order to explain how humans left the state of nature and entered different stages of civilization. He emphasizes the role of the passions, which precede the capacity for reason. According to Rousseau, it 'is by the activity of our passions, that our reason improves: … it is impossible to conceive, why a man exempt from fears and desires should take the trouble to reason' (Rousseau 2002: 97). His view of individual development reflects his understanding of historical development. The passions constitute an important topic in *Emile* (1762), where the tutor is keen on regulating the passions Emile experiences. Rousseau emphasizes that of all the faculties, 'reason, which is, so to speak, only a composite of all the others, is the one that develops with the most difficulty and latest' (Rousseau 1979: 89). He criticizes other educational writers, naming John Locke, for having assumed children to be reasoning creatures at too early an age and for wanting to develop reason in order to regulate the passions. This is, according to Rousseau, to 'begin with the end, to want to make the product the instrument' (Rousseau 1979: 89). Reason is a product of the passions and therefore cannot regulate them; young children, particularly, have not yet developed a capacity for reasoning. Instead, the passions have to be regulated from the outside, so to say, by regulating impressions and thus guarding the child from harmful incitements and giving rise to beneficial ones.

Wollstonecraft and Rousseau agree that the passions provide necessary motives, without which humans would not exercise their capacity for reason, but they hold different conceptions of reason, which affects their evaluation of the passions.[16] When Rousseau emphasizes that reason is a slowly developing derivative faculty, he is explicitly criticizing the majority of his predecessors and contemporaries, who claim that reason is an innate capacity, which by its very existence in the human mind distinguishes humans from other animals (Rousseau 2002: 95–6). As we have seen, Wollstonecraft belongs to this majority and her view affects, among many things, her view on how children are taught to regulate their passions. In *Thoughts on the Education of Daughters* (1787), most likely written before Wollstonecraft read Rousseau's *Emile*,[17] she recommends that educators 'follow Mr Locke's system' and states that though the 'understanding ... should not be overloaded any more than the stomach', reasoning does constitute an important part of this system (*Works* 4: 9–10). Not unlike Rousseau, Wollstonecraft holds that it is 'the duty of a parent to preserve a child from receiving wrong impressions' (*Works* 4: 11), but this protective strategy of negative education must be complemented by an early activation of reason. Like Locke, she thinks that children should 'be permitted to enter into conversations' even if 'it requires great discernment to find out such subjects as will gradually improve them'. Whenever 'a child asks a question, it should always have a reasonable answer given it' (*Works* 4: 10; also Locke 1964: § 81, 65–6).[18] In this way, Wollstonecraft continues, the child's 'little passions should be engaged' (*Works* 4: 10). Here we see a close interchange between reason and passion, where Wollstonecraft seems to think that the way the two strengthen each other is benevolent.

There are no indications that Wollstonecraft's view changes after she has read *Emile* and writes *Rights of Woman*. In the later book, we find her discussing how the heart and the understanding must be cultivated together. She points out that 'perhaps, in the education of both sexes, the most difficult task is so to adjust instruction as not to narrow the understanding, whilst the heart is warmed by the generous juices of spring ... nor to dry up the feelings by employing the mind in investigations remote from life' (*Works* 5: 135). The problems Wollstonecraft

---

[16] For more detail on Rousseau's view and how it differs from Wollstonecraft's, see Reuter (2017).

[17] It is likely that *Thoughts on the Education of Daughters* was finished before Wollstonecraft left London to work as a governess in Ireland. She tells her sister Everina that she is reading *Emile* in a letter from Dublin dated 24 March 1787 (*Letters*: 113–15), but it is of course possible that she was familiar with the book even before that.

[18] For Rousseau's criticism of reasoning with children, see Rousseau (1979: 90).

identifies, as well as many of her suggested remedies, are close to those discussed by Rousseau. He too warns against engaging the young mind in investigations remote from life (e.g. Rousseau 1979: 177). They differ most on the relation between reason and passion. Wollstonecraft is less worried than Rousseau that 'the generous juices of spring' may corrupt rather than strengthen young people's understanding. She argues this is so because from the very beginning, even when it is only starting to develop in young children, reason is independent and not a derivative of other mental capacities. Humans have an innate capacity for reason independent of the passions, but the passions are necessary auxiliaries of reason in the sense that without the passions, humans would not reason, that is, use their capacity for reason. Wollstonecraft's belief in the independence and strength of reason allows her to give the passions free rein even when they provide false views of life. Her understanding of the strength and providential role of reason also allows her to take a more optimistic view of civilization than Rousseau does.

3.2 Strong Passions, Sublime Emotions and Generous Feeling

When discussing the effects of the passions on women's lives, Wollstonecraft points out that 'it is not against strong preserving passions; but romantic wavering feelings that I wish to guard the female heart' (*Works* 5: 143). In her vocabulary, the passions are predominantly grand, strong and persistent, whereas feelings and sentiments tend to be weak and wavering. Amy Schmitter reminds us that Wollstonecraft relates sentiment to sensuality, as when she refers to 'the fallacious light of sentiment; too often used as a softer phrase for sensuality' (*Works* 5: 115; Schmitter 2013: 207). Passions prompt humans to act as well as think, whereas feelings and sentiments belong to feminized passivity. Wollstonecraft condemns the 'sensualists', who 'cherish ... weakness under the name of delicacy', and contrasts the desire these sensualists feel for the weakened beings of their own creation with the 'sublime emotions' inspired by women who display true 'intellectual beauty' (*Works* 5: 116).

'Sublime emotions' are also felt towards God. Discussing the question of why 'the gracious fountain of life give[s] us passions', Wollstonecraft asks why the Creator should 'lead us from love of ourselves to the sublime emotions which the discovery of his wisdom and goodness excites, if these feelings are not set in motion to improve our nature, of which they make a part' (*Works* 5: 84). Sublime emotions contain an element of respect, which human intellectual beauty can evoke, as can the wisdom and goodness of God. The concept of 'the sublime' was well established in British philosophical terminology by the time

Wollstonecraft was writing. As we can see from her usage, the sublime had strong moral and aesthetic connotations. Following the early eighteenth-century work of Joseph Addison, the experience of greatness was related to an enlargement of the soul itself (Guyer 2013: 407). Sublime emotions enlarge the soul and so, in the moral context given by Wollstonecraft, these emotions are not focused on petty self-interest, but on the good of others and ultimately on the highest good, God.

Wollstonecraft's account of how humans are led by their Creator 'from love of ourselves to the sublime emotions which the discovery of his wisdom and goodness excites' (*Works* 5: 84) shows that passions and feelings are part of human nature and not only to be struggled against, but also to be transformed into higher forms of emotion. Wollstonecraft describes a continuum, beginning with self-love and developing into a sublime love of (God's) wisdom. Her continuum resembles the transformative ladder of love in Plato's *Symposium* (206a–212b), and justifies claims about Wollstonecraft's Platonism. In this case, her source is not Price's Platonist metaphysics and epistemology, but rather John Milton's Platonist love poetry. In *Rights of Men*, Wollstonecraft makes a direct reference to Plato and Milton when she argues against what she sees as Edmund Burke's idealized picture of women's 'beautiful weakness'. She claims that if Burke is right, it would mean 'that Plato and Milton were grossly mistaken in asserting that human love led to heavenly, and was only an exaltation of the same affection; for the love of the Deity, which is mixed with the most profound reverence, must be love of perfection, and not compassion for weakness' (*Works* 5: 46).

Wollstonecraft makes it clear that lower forms of love can develop into higher forms and, most importantly, that these are forms of 'the same affection' throughout. She uses a Platonist emphasis on the close relation between the true, the good and the beautiful to criticize Burke's distinction between the beautiful and the sublime.[19] In his influential *A Philosophical Inquiry into the Origin of Our Ideas of the Sublime and the Beautiful* (1757), Burke connects the pleasures of beauty with feelings of love, including sexual desire, affection and tenderness. These feelings are relaxing, but less intense than the feelings invoked by sublime

---

[19] On the theological implications of Wollstonecraft's criticism of Burke's distinction between the sublime and the beautiful, see Emily Dumler-Winckler, who argues that this distinction, in combination with his account of religious experience as paradigmatically sublime, makes it 'incredibly difficult to simultaneously revere and love God' (Dumler-Winckler 2019: 301). Wollstonecraft's criticism resembles Anna Letitia Barbauld's theological views as expressed in her *Devotional Pieces* (1775). Barbauld, a rational dissenter critical of the strictly rationalist theology of Joseph Priestley and Price, writes that the seat of devotion is in 'the imagination and the passions, and it has its source in that relish for the sublime, the vast, and the beautiful'; cited in Smith (2019: 53).

objects, which include an element of fear (Guyer 2013: 407–10). In Wollstonecraft's usage, true beauty seems to acquire features of greatness, usually associated with the sublime. She is not identifying the two concepts, but arguing that if love of beauty is to guide humans towards love of truth and the moral good, beauty cannot be mere desirable or affectionate weakness. Likewise, the sublime cannot be mere astonishment or the pleasure of watching terror at a safe distance. In *An Historical and Moral View of the French Revolution* (1794), when questioning the moral impact of ancient tragedies, she writes: 'The sublime terrour [*sic*], with which they fill the mind, may amuse, nay, delight; but whence comes the improvement? Besides, uncultivated minds are the most subject to feel astonishment, which is often only another name for sublime sensations' (*Works* 6: 112).

Neither beauty reduced to mere delicacy nor sublimity reduced to astonishing terror can guide moral development, but this does not mean that beauty and the sublime are not in themselves potentially valuable. Wollstonecraft is not dividing passions, feelings and emotions into categories of bad and good. They are all good in the sense that they are part of human nature created by God. The crucial question is how humans react upon them and use them as part of their moral lives. 'Feelings' are given strong positive connotations when Wollstonecraft discusses 'generous feeling'. The context is worth citing in full:

> I descend from my height, and mixing with my fellow-creatures, feel myself hurried along the common stream; ambition, love, hope, and fear, exert their wonted power, though we be convinced by reason that their present and most attractive promises are only lying dreams; but had the cold hand of circumspection damped each generous feeling before it had left any permanent character, or fixed some habit, what could be expected, but selfish prudence and reason just rising above instinct? Who that has read Dean Swift's disgusting description of the Yahoos, and insipid one of Houyhnhnm with a philosophical eye, can avoid seeing the futility of degrading the passions, or making man rest in contentment? (*Works* 5: 181)

Here we find the familiar description of how the passions activate reason and work for the good even when the goals they present are false, but we also find an explicit criticism of reason as it appears when unaffected by passion. 'Generous feeling' is in itself a necessary good, not only an auxiliary to reason. The description of 'reason just rising above instinct' is reminiscent of Wollstonecraft's remark in her *Hints*, where she claims that 'the deductions of reason destroy sublimity' (*Works* 5: 274). Wollstonecraft's reference to Jonathan Swift's Stoic Houyhnhnm and desire-driven Yahoos is in many respects interesting. Swift's *Gulliver's Travels* (1726) is, among other things, a satirical criticism of Stoicism, including its conception of *apatheia*. The Houyhnhnm express friendship and benevolence towards 'the whole Race' (Swift 2005: 250), but remain indifferent towards particular individuals and do not show signs of grief when loved ones die (Swift 2005: 256).[20]

Wollstonecraft seems to agree with Swift's satire of Stoic ideals. We can distinguish two aspects of her criticism. First, Wollstonecraft thinks that we have to have generous feelings towards particular human beings in order to develop similar feelings on an abstract or universal level. Alluding to the Gospel of John (4: 20) as well as the Platonist ladder of love, she asks: 'He who loves not his brother whom he hath seen, how can he love God?' (*Works* 5: 177). The idea of beings who feel universal benevolence, but do not grieve at the death of their children, is a paradox.

Second, Wollstonecraft criticizes the very ideal of contentment. When she discusses how the passions nourished by false views of life exercise human reason and judgement, she adds that thereby we are 'permitted to overleap the boundary that secures content' (*Works* 5: 179). Contentment threatens the motivating force of the passions. Wollstonecraft continues by asking: 'if, in the dawn of life, we could soberly survey the scenes before as in perspective, and see every thing in its true colours, how could the passions gain sufficient strength to unfold the faculties?' (*Works* 5: 179). We may want to read Wollstonecraft's remark as exclusively concerning the moral development of young people, but this does not seem to hold. She does think that most people need the motivating force of the passions throughout their adult lives. Humans are perfectible beings, who must aim to perfect themselves, but they must also stay aware that they are created imperfect. The ideal of a perfectly wise sage, who sees everything in its true colours, is not achievable. Not for humans in this world, at least.

Wollstonecraft does not discuss Stoicism in any detail, but Macaulay's *Letters on Education* includes three chapters on the Stoics.[21] In her review of the book, Wollstonecraft writes that the 'doctrines of the Stoics are clearly stated by Mrs M. and some unjust aspersions wiped off, which bigotry and ignorance have industriously propagated, to render doctrines ridiculous or odious, which deserve respect' (*Works* 7: 320). Macaulay aims at reconciling Stoicism with Christianity and she argues that Stoicism was about as good a moral system as can be 'independent of the pleasing and encouraging hope afforded by the Christian revelation' (Macaulay 1996: 442). Her main criticism concerns the

---

[20] I discuss the characteristics of the Houyhnhnms and Yahoos and their significance for Wollstonecraft at greater length in Reuter (2016).

[21] Macaulay's interest in Stoicism may have been influenced by Elisabeth Carter's English translation of Epictetus' works, first published in 1758. For a discussion of Carter's and Macaulay's views on Stoicism, see Hutton (2007).

ideal of self-sufficiency. The problem with 'the doctrine of the stoics, proceed[s] from their considering the infirm and dependent creature, man, in the light of a self sufficient independent being' (Macaulay 1996: 452). Wollstonecraft would agree with Macaulay's criticism of self-sufficiency, which illuminates the problem with the ideal of contentment.[22] In order to be truly content, a being has to be – or at least feel – self-sufficient. Yet humans are not self-sufficient and the feeling of contentment is therefore illusory. It is not only a question of being a dependent creature, but of being aware of this fact. Animals, who do not strive for an afterlife, may very well feel content when they have satisfied their instinctual desires, but the human lot is different, since humans are capable of improvement (e.g. *Works* 4: 372). The capacity for improvement involves reason, passion and, as we will see next, imagination.

4 Imagination

Wollstonecraft attends to the imagination throughout her literary career. Scholars have given this a fair amount of attention. John Whale's study of imagination and futurity in Wollstonecraft's thought is particularly worth mentioning.[23] The imagination makes it possible to perceive what is not present, including what might conceivably be possible in the future. Contrary to reason, which may also perceive what is not present, the imagination paints pictures of the non-present and makes humans either desire or fear non-present things. Whale discusses future states in the context of Wollstonecraft's religion as well as her understanding of revolution and the progress of history. Importantly, his discussion of Wollstonecraft's sources points at the likely influence of Jacques Necker's *De l'Importance des Opinions Religieuses*, which she translated for Joseph Johnson in 1788. Necker emphasizes the role of imagination in religious experience, where it lends 'a new force to religious sentiments' (*Works* 3: 26). Comparing imagination and reason, Necker argues, in Wollstonecraft's translation, that 'our imagination is less restrained, and the minutest description of reason can never equal in power, the lively and

---

[22] Wollstonecraft thinks that the Stoics deserve respect, as we saw, but in the light of her overall view on the passions, it is likely that had she studied Stoicism more closely, her conclusions would have been more critical than Macaulay's. Their difference on the passions is illuminated by another passage in the review, where Wollstonecraft questions what she takes to be Macaulay's overtly stern view on the passions and writes, in line with what we have seen, that it 'may be necessary for the passions to be felt before their operations can be understood' (*Works* 7: 313). Richard Vernon has interestingly argued that Wollstonecraft's understanding of the universal and thus gender-neutral character of morality is compatible with and perhaps loosely influenced by Stoicism, but he is wrong when he claims that 'Wollstonecraft pursues [the] ancient theme of non-attachment vigorously and systematically' (Vernon 2005: 61).

[23] See Whale (2000). Other studies discussing Wollstonecraft's views on the imagination are Green (1997); Khin Zaw (1998); Taylor (2003); Reuter (2017); and Tomaselli (2021: 81–91).

impulsive ardour of the affections of our souls' (*Works* 3: 26). The significance of this motive force is not only religious. 'For Necker', Whale writes, 'it is important that imagination is a spur to moral action and that it is never self-satisfied by gratification in the present moment' (Whale 2000: 74). As we will see in Subsection 4.2, imagination's role as a spur to action is essential to Wollstonecraft's criticism of contentment and to her views on human improvement.

In Wollstonecraft's system of thought, imagination plays a role in religion, politics, morality, aesthetics and philosophy of the mind. She draws on the lively interest in the imagination that developed throughout the eighteenth century, not least among British authors. Joseph Addison published eleven essays on 'The Pleasures of the Imagination' in the *Spectator* in 1712. These essays were followed by an intensive attention to what would later be called experiences of aesthetic qualities, focusing on questions of taste, the beautiful and the sublime (Guyer 2013). Towards the second half of the century, interest in the pleasures of imagination was accompanied by a growing awareness of its creative role. Authors such as Alexander Gerard and William Duff single out 'the imagination as the seat of genius' (Kivy 2013: 481). Wollstonecraft acknowledges both roles of imagination, and she is particularly interested in its creative potential. In her case, creative imagination is not limited to geniuses. Just like reason, it is a mental capacity distinctive of human beings and in need of exercise. When appropriately exercised, the imagination essentially shapes the moral person. In Subsection 4.1, I discuss the scope of the imagination and in Subsection 4.2, I discuss its motive force.

4.1 The Scope of the Imagination

There is a close connection between the imagination and the passions. In *Discourse on the Origin and Foundations of Inequality Among Mankind*, Rousseau argues that the imagination distinguishes human passions from passions caused by physical needs, which humans share with other animals. In the state of nature, the desires of savage man 'never extend beyond his physical wants; He knows no goods but food, a female, and rest; he fears no evils but pain, and hunger; . . . His imagination paints nothing to him; his heart asks nothing from him' (Rousseau 2002: 97). Civilization starts with the unfolding of the imagination, and Rousseau names fear of death and curiosity as two new features that begin to affect human lives. The imagination creates new passions by creating new objects of fear and desire. As in the case of reason, Rousseau draws parallels between the passions' historical and individual development. In *Emile*, the regulation of the passions and imagination go hand in hand. Rousseau writes: 'As soon as [the child's] potential faculties are put in action, imagination, the most active of all, is awakened and outstrips them. It is imagination which extends for us the measure of the possible, whether for good or bad, and which consequently excites and nourishes the desires by the hope of satisfying them' (Rousseau 1979: 80–1).

The problem is that the 'imaginary world is infinite' whereas the 'real world has its limits' (Rousseau 1979: 81). The imagination raises desires that cannot even in principle be satisfied. Imagination must be regulated in order to fit the finite world, but regulation must not simply suppress development. If desires were simply diminished, 'a part of our faculties would remain idle, and we would not enjoy our whole being' (Rousseau 1979: 80). Education must aim at 'diminishing the excess of the desires . . . and putting power and will in perfect equality' (Rousseau 1979: 80). Throughout *Emile*, Rousseau describes a delicate balance between encouraging the imagination in the right direction – as when Emile and Sophie are led to fall in love with each other – and preventing it from painting pictures of the unachievable. A similar balancing act guides Rousseau's views on the ideal development of civilization and political society. One of the aims of his *The Social Contract* is to balance human freedom and the necessities of self-preservation (e.g. Rousseau 2002: 163).

We find many similarities between Rousseau's and Wollstonecraft's views on the imagination. One of these is the idea that the imagination is a distinctly human faculty. We saw in Subsection 2.2 that according to Wollstonecraft, animals lack the capacity to improve themselves. This is because they lack both reason and imagination. In *Original Stories*, she writes: 'The birds you saw today do not improve – or their improvement only tends to self-preservation; the first nest they make and the last are exactly the same; though in their flights they must see many others more beautiful if not more convenient, and, had they reason, they would probably shew something like individual taste in the form of their dwellings; but this is not the case' (*Works* 4: 372).

Wollstonecraft draws the conclusion that 'we neither see imagination nor wisdom' in animals (*Works* 4: 372). The passage is interesting, not least because it points at a close connection between reason, taste and imagination. In this early work, Wollstonecraft holds that taste depends on reason as well as the imagination. In some of her posthumously published writings, she portrays imagination as a capacity which is even more distinctly human than reason. In the *Hints*, she emphasizes that though 'reason in this world is the mother of wisdom – yet some flights of the imagination seem to reach what wisdom cannot teach – and while they delude us here, afford a glorious hope, if not a foretaste, of what we may expect hereafter' (*Works* 5: 274). Here we see the connection to futurity. Wollstonecraft describes the imagination as a vehicle for religious experience and as such as a necessary addition to the worldly wisdom provided by reason. The passage concludes by claiming that 'the deductions of reason destroy sublimity' (*Works* 5: 274). Here sublimity stands for the grandness of God and the afterlife, which the imagination can perceive, but which transcends reason and is destroyed by the pettiness of deductive reasoning.

Wollstonecraft mentions the imagination several times in her letters to her lover Gilbert Imlay. Here the imagination is closely related to moral and aesthetic values. In a letter dated in Paris in September 1794 she writes:

> Believe me, sage sir, you have not sufficient respect for the imagination – I could prove to you in a trice that it is the mother of sentiment, the great distinction of our nature, the only purifier of the passions – animals have a portion of reason, and equal, if not more exquisite, senses; but no trace of imagination, or her offspring taste, appears in any of their actions. The impulse of the senses, passions, if you will, and the conclusions of reason, draw men together; but the imagination is the true fire, stolen from heaven, to animate this cold creature of clay, producing all those fine sympathies that lead to rapture, rendering men social by expanding their hearts, instead of leaving them leisure to calculate how many comforts society affords.
>
> (*Letters*: 264)

Wollstonecraft's remark on animals having a portion of reason contradicts her outspoken view in *Rights of Woman* that 'man's pre-eminence over the brute creation consist[s] ... in Reason' (*Works* 5: 81). In order to understand her philosophical intentions, we need to consider her discussion on the limitations of reason. The 'portion of reason' that animals may have, which 'draw men together' and 'calculate ... comforts', is instrumental reason, aiming for material self-preservation and self-satisfaction. This is the 'reason just rising above instinct' to which Wollstonecraft refers in the context of Swift's Yahoos and Houyhnhnm (*Works* 5: 181).[24] As we saw in that passage, reason must be accompanied by 'generous feeling' in order for morality to become more than 'selfish prudence' (*Works* 5: 181). Imagination, for its part, is instrumental in producing generous feeling. In a letter to Imlay dated in June 1795, Wollstonecraft adds: 'Ah! my friend, you know not the ineffable delight, the exquisite pleasure, which arises from a unison of affection and desire, when the whole soul and senses are abandoned to a lively imagination, that renders every emotion delicate and rapturous' (*Letters*: 297).

The imagination is a 'purifier of the passions', which renders 'emotion delicate' and produces 'fine sympathies' (*Letters*: 264, 297). Here we need to

---

[24] It is the kind of reason that Swift attributes to the Yahoos; see Swift (2005: 231).

ask how Wollstonecraft's view on emotions purified by the imagination relates to theories of moral sense and moral sentiments. Many eighteenth-century British – and in particular Scottish – authors discussing taste established that it had an affinity with moral sense. Francis Hutcheson's *Inquiry into the Original of Our Ideas of Beauty and Virtue* (1725) is a well-known example. The book is divided into two parts: the first discusses beauty and the second, virtue. Paul Guyer emphasizes that Hutcheson's strategy was to use 'the presumably non-controversial existence of a "sense of beauty" to prepare the way for the acceptance of a more controversial "moral sense"' (Guyer 2013: 398). Hutcheson did cause controversy. Richard Price uses Hutcheson as the prime example in his criticism of moral sense theory. Price does not accept the possibility that 'our ideas of morality ... have the same original with our ideas of the sensible qualities of bodies, the harmony of sounds, or the beauties of painting or sculpture' (Price 1758: 12). He is particularly worried about moral sense being a faculty distinct from reason. Price argues that if morality is 'a thing equally steady, independent, and unchangeable with *all truth*', then ideas of right and wrong, like other truths, must be perceived by the understanding or, in other words, reason (Price 1758: 15, 17). He affiliates morality with knowledge, not with taste.

Wollstonecraft defends a moral realism that has much in common with Price's view (see Subsection 7.1). There are no reasons to suppose that she changed her mind about the foundation of morality when she was emphasizing the imagination and passions, but her moral epistemology and her understanding of moral motivation differ from Price's strict rationalism and his doctrine of innate ideas (see Subsection 6.2). Price's remarks on the imagination illustrate the difference between their views. He holds that the imagination is 'a faculty nearly allied to *sense*' (Price 1758: 26). From the close affinity with sense, it follows that 'the conceptions of the imagination' are 'rude and gross, falling *infinitely* short of that certainty, accuracy, universality, and clearness, which belong to *intellectual discernment*' (Price 1758: 29–30). Price is a classical Platonist, who emphasizes the real existence of universal ideas known by reason. The imagination produces ideas that are rude and gross because they come from mere particular beings. 'All that can be pictured in the imagination', he writes, 'is indeed particular' (Price 1758: 43).

Wollstonecraft disagrees with Price's first two claims about the imagination and revaluates the third. Like most eighteenth-century writers, she emphasizes the difference rather than the affinity between sense and imagination. The imagination is a 'purifier' of passions and sense perceptions. She writes to Imlay that 'senses are abandoned to a lively imagination' (*Letters*: 297). Far from being rude and gross, as she writes in the *Hints*, 'some flights of the imagination seem to reach what wisdom cannot teach' (*Works* 5: 274). Finally, Wollstonecraft emphasizes the need to perceive particulars. As we saw in Subsection 3.2: 'He who loves not his brother whom he hath seen, how can he love God?' (*Works* 5: 177). Wollstonecraft shares the basics of Price's Platonist metaphysics of universals, but she follows a different branch of the Platonist tradition, which was influenced by Plato's *Symposium* and *Phaedrus* and where 'the ladder of love', reaching through particulars towards universals, plays an important role.

Even when emphasizing that the passions and imagination are important, Wollstonecraft does not posit a moral sense distinct from reason. We will see in Sections 6 and 7 that she upholds a strong connection between morality and truth as well as between knowledge and virtue. Still, she does think that the passions – and in particular passions purified by the imagination – are a 'necessary auxiliary of reason' (*Works* 5: 16). The branch of Platonism that inspires her emphasizes the close affinity between the ideas of truth, the good and the beautiful. This means that questions of morality, taste and knowledge are related. Wollstonecraft is very critical of a conflation of taste and morality, but she does think that when treated correctly, taste may have moral value. When discussing the educational role of novels in *Rights of Woman*, she writes that 'even the productions that are only addressed to the imagination, raise the reader a little above the gross gratification of appetites, to which the mind has not given a shade of delicacy' (*Works* 5: 256). Here Wollstonecraft gives educational and moral credit to Addison's 'pleasures of the imagination'. She distances herself, not only from Price's views, but also from Macaulay's *Letters on Education* and Rousseau's *Emile*. In her review, Wollstonecraft agrees that Macaulay's 'remarks upon some celebrated novels are just', but adds as her opinion 'that we should not so widely deviate from nature, as not to allow the imagination to forage a little for the judgment' (*Works* 7: 313). Rousseau, for his part, is (in)famous for his negative attitude towards books in general: 'The child who reads does not think, he only reads' (Rousseau 1979: 168). In Rousseau's view, books are problematic because, like the imagination, they mediate reality and substitute the world as it is with mere representation.[25] Wollstonecraft is aware of the problems of delusion, but she takes a more optimistic stance than Rousseau does, not least when on the motive force of the imagination.

---

[25] Still, Rousseau does not condemn all books. Daniel Defoe's *Robinson Crusoe* (1719) plays an important part in Emile's education, and François Fénelon's *Les Aventures de Télémaque* (1699) has a similar function in the education of Sophie. In both cases these books are recommended because they have a beneficial impact on the imagination of their respective readers. For more detail, see Reuter (2017: 1144–5), including the references.

4.2 Imagination as Motive Force

Many eighteenth-century authors identify a tension between human content-ment and the imagination's infinite ability to posit new goals, but there are different evaluations of this tension. We saw that Rousseau finds the infinite scope of the imagination problematic. In *Emile*, he describes the motivating force of imaginary objects:

> [T]he object which first appeared to be at hand flees more quickly than it can be pursued. When one believes that one has reached it, it transforms and reveals itself in the distance ahead of us. No longer seeing the country we have already crossed, we count it for nothing; what remains to cross cease-lessly grows and extends. Thus one exhausts oneself without getting to the end, and the more one gains on enjoyment, the further happiness gets from us.
>
> (Rousseau 1979: 81)

In Rousseau's view, the workings of the imagination threaten human happiness understood as contentment. He claims that in order to be happy one must be 'content with the present hour' (Rousseau 1979: 411) and he uses a metaphor of space to describe the chase after imaginary objects. Interestingly, we find a similar language of space in Wollstonecraft's translation of Necker's *Importance of Religious Opinions*. Necker describes how 'it is always easy to move' a person, when 'we address ourselves to his imagination'. He goes on to claim that 'this faculty of our mind excites us continually to action, by presenting to our eyes a great space, and by keeping us always at a certain distance from the object we have in view' (*Works* 3: 26). The imagination is not without risk as it may inflame 'mere credulous faith in superstitious opinions' (*Works* 3: 26), but Necker's remedy is not to curb, but rather to use it in religious education and direct the imagination towards the all-powerful God. In the right context, in contrast to Rousseau's fears, the 'great space' and 'distance from the object' turn out to be beneficial.

Wollstonecraft, finally, uses a similar metaphor of space to describe the workings of the imagination in her 'Letter on the Present Character of the French Nation' (1793).[26] She writes:

> The wants of reason are very few, and, were we to consider dispassionately the real value of most things, we should probably rest satisfied with the simple gratification of our physical necessities, and be content with negative goodness: for it is frequently, only that wanton, the Imagination, with her artful coquetry, who lures us forward, and makes us run over a rough road, pushing aside every obstacle merely to catch a disappointment. (*Works* 6: 445)

---

[26] Wollstonecraft wrote this soon after her arrival in Paris, and the letter was intended to be the first in a published series. The series was not continued, and the letter was first published as part of her posthumous works, edited by Godwin.

On the surface, Wollstonecraft seems to agree with Rousseau that the imagination is a wanton, which causes unhappiness. Such an interpretation misses
Wollstonecraft's irony, and with it the core of her argument.[27] In
Subsection 3.1.2, we saw that she uses a similar metaphor of space when she
argues that the passions are necessary auxiliaries of reason: 'a present impulse
pushes us forward, and when we discover that the game did not deserve the
chase, we find that we have gone over much ground, and not only gained many
new ideas, but a habit of thinking' (*Works* 5: 16). We may catch mere disap-
pointments, but the chase itself is not in vain. The passage in the 'Letter' must
be read in relation to Wollstonecraft's general criticism of contentment, which
is, crucially, present also in the 'Letter'. Wollstonecraft takes a critical view of
the French. She describes her impressions:

> On all sides they trip along, buoyed up by animal spirits, and seemingly so
> void of care, that often, when I am walking on the *Boulevards*, it occurs to me,
> that they alone understand the full import of the term leisure; and that they
> trifle their time away with such an air of contentment, I know not how to wish
> them wiser at the expence of their gaiety. (*Works* 6: 443)

The French are described as 'the most sensual people in the world' (*Works* 6:
444). In Paris, the 'soul of Epicurus has long been at work' and the minds of
people have become 'cold and artificial by the selfish enjoyments of the senses'
(*Works* 6: 445).[28] The search for mere contentment and sensual gratification is,
according to Wollstonecraft, characteristic of people lacking imagination. In
one of her letters to Imlay, Wollstonecraft writes that men with 'gross appetites,
must have variety to banish *ennui*, because the imagination never lends its
magic wand to convert appetite into love' (*Letters*: 297). Sensual appetites
occasionally threaten contentment, or as Wollstonecraft also calls it 'satiety'
(*Letters*: 297), but in the long run they are compatible, because appetites can be
gratified. This is the state described in 'Letter on the Character of the French
Nation', where we can 'rest satisfied with the simple gratification of our
physical necessities, and be content with negative goodness' (*Works* 6: 445).
It is animal contentment, the satisfaction of physical needs and the absence of
suffering, but for humans, it cannot be the goal. As we saw in Subsection 3.2,
Wollstonecraft's criticism of contentment reminds us of Macaulay's criticism of

---

[27] Tomaselli acknowledges this passage, which is often overlooked by scholars, but she interprets it as
a criticism of the imagination inspired by 'the events [Wollstonecraft] witnessed under the Terror'
(Tomaselli 2021: 85). Tomaselli's interpretation does not fit the nature of Wollstonecraft's criticism
of the French.

[28] There is no doubt that Wollstonecraft's description is based more on British prejudice against the
French than on her observations in Paris, but we do not need to bother about whether her claims
are true. Our concern focuses on her description of contentment and its relation to the
imagination.

the Stoic ideal of self-sufficiency. The Stoics famously aim not to suffer, and in the passages under discussion, Wollstonecraft contrasts the imagination both with striving for mere 'negative goodness', that is, the absence of suffering, and with mere sensual gratification, attributed to the Epicureans, whom she (like many of her contemporaries) associated with materialism and sensuality. Wollstonecraft finds neither of the two ancient schools satisfactory, though she clearly has more sympathy for Stoicism than for Epicureanism as she understood it.

Humans must strive for positive goodness, and even if the imagination may delude them, it is essential to this human task. The imagination alone produces emotions 'over which satiety has no power' (*Letters*: 297). As in the case of the passions, Wollstonecraft values the imagination both in itself – despite the fact that it may present delusionary goals – and in a more qualified sense, due to the valuable goals it can present when put to correct use. The imagination is in many respects 'the true fire, stolen from heaven' (*Letters*: 264). It is potentially dangerous and has to be handled with care, but it is essential to human perfectibility. Appetites may be satisfied, but reason never reaches its goal: ultimate perfection. Reason on its own remains 'cold', though, and the imagination is a necessary auxiliary, which must accompany reason in its search for truth and virtue. It is crucial that the imagination, as Necker writes, is 'keeping us always at a certain distance from the object we have in view' (*Works* 3: 26). The imagination keeps us going even though we are aiming for perfections we can never reach.

Wollstonecraft seems to give the imagination at least two separate roles, even if she does not explicitly distinguish them. First, like the passions, the imagination exercises the mental capacities and initiates human action in general. Here the goals may well be delusive, but the imagination is not without value, not least because it resists contentment. Second, the imagination may spur humans to act on particular goals set by reason, virtue or faith. In these cases, the goals themselves are independent of the imagination, but the imagination contributes to their articulation.

There is in particular one passage in *Rights of Woman* where Wollstonecraft describes how the imagination works. She discusses why women, who are 'seldom absolutely alone', fall prey to sentiments rather than developing passions of higher value: 'Solitude and reflection are necessary to give to wishes the force of passions, and to enable the imagination to enlarge the object, and make it the most desirable' (*Works* 5: 127).[29] We can illustrate Wollstonecraft's

---

[29] The passage is an interesting forerunner to Virginia Woolf's argument that a woman needs a room of her own to write (Woolf 1989).

point with an example. Let us say that I wish to write a book. I will need solitude and reflection in order to imagine my goal in such a way that my mere wish becomes an action-inciting passion. In this case, the goal may be said to exist independently of the imagination, but it is obviously transformed in the process of becoming my most desirable goal. When enlarged by the imagination, the goal of writing a book may be experienced as more *real* than it was when it remained a mere wish. The experience of realness is related to the imagination's ability to 'paint pictures', or particularize objects, and strengthens the desire to gain the object or goal in question.

The imagination's ability to particularize is especially important in the case of abstract objects and goals. This is why Wollstonecraft considers the imagination so important to religion. In the *Hints*, she claims that the imagination affords 'a glorious hope, if not a foretaste, of what we may expect hereafter' (*Works* 5: 274) and in *Rights of Woman*, she discusses how a beloved object 'seen through the medium of the imagination' can teach 'to love the centre of all perfection' (*Works* 5: 180). Humans have to imagine God in order to properly adore and love God. The imagination particularizes God, who nevertheless remains a transcendent being that, in accordance with Necker's view of the imagination, must be pursued even though God can never be reached (*Works* 3: 26). Wollstonecraft's examples where the imagination particularizes abstract entities are mostly related to religion, but she applies similar dynamics to morality and politics. Imagining a just society strengthens our desire to pursue it and may affect our understanding of what a just society looks like. We saw in Subsection 4.1 that the imagination is able to render 'men social by expanding their hearts' (*Letters*: 264). Because of its relations with sociability and moral emotions, the imagination plays a crucial role in Wollstonecraft's discussions of love and friendship.

5 Love and Friendship

Wollstonecraft's discussions of love and friendship summarize her views on reason, passion and imagination. She presents a complex relationship between what she conceives to be two grand human affections, which are in some respects allied, but also opposites. In *Rights of Woman*, Wollstonecraft famously writes that:

> Friendship is a serious affection; the most sublime of all affections, because it is founded on principle, and cemented by time. The very reverse may be said of love. In a great degree, love and friendship cannot subsist in the same bosom; even when inspired by different objects they weaken or destroy each other, and for the same object can only be felt in succession. The vain fears

and fond jealousies, the winds which fan the flame of love, when judiciously or artfully tempered, are both incompatible with the tender confidence and sincere respect of friendship. (*Works* 5: 142)

The passage summarizes several of Wollstonecraft's claims about love and friendship. Friendship is a sublime affection, which, as we saw in Subsection 3.2, indicates that friendship enlarges the soul. It is based on principle, which here equals principles of reason. Towards the end of *Rights of Woman*, Wollstonecraft writes that 'reason must cement friendship' (*Works* 5: 261). Since friendship is an affection cemented by reason and time, it is not only an affection, but also to be considered as one of 'the fairest virtues' (*Works* 5: 23), as Wollstonecraft writes in *Rights of Men*. Most importantly, friendship can exist only among equals. In *Rights of Men*, she writes that 'true happiness arose from the friendship and intimacy which can only be enjoyed by equals' (*Works* 5: 10–11). Wollstonecraft's emphasis on equality as the necessary basis of friendship, repeated in *Rights of Woman* (*Works* 5: 241), constitutes the radical core of her conception of marriage as friendship. Partners in marriage have to be equal in order to be friends.

Wollstonecraft describes love and friendship as two distinct emotions that 'cannot subsist in the same bosom'. She portrays love as an incorporation of unstable feeling, the opposite of stable friendship. Contrary to friendship, love is not, in this passage, to be considered a virtue. Still, there can be a continuum between the two, in which case they are 'felt in succession'. According to Wollstonecraft, love may develop into stable friendship. One important aspect of her view, not least according to many modern commentators, concerns the question of what happens to sexual desire when love develops into friendship (e.g. Abbey 1999: 80).

Wollstonecraft's views on love and friendship have gained a considerable amount of attention, beginning with William Godwin's biography of his late wife, *Memoirs of the Author of 'The Rights of Woman'* (1798) and his publication of her letters to Gilbert Imlay. Describing Wollstonecraft's romantic involvement with Imlay, Godwin writes in the *Memoirs* that she 'nourished an individual affection, which she saw no necessity of subjecting to restraint; and a heart like hers was not formed to nourish affection by halves' (Godwin 1987: 242). Godwin's biographical approach and his emphasis on Wollstonecraft's passionate personality are echoed in early twentieth-century feminist reflections on her life and work, such as essays by Emma Goldman (1911) and Virginia Woolf (1929).[30] Some late twentieth-century feminist

---

[30] For modern editions of these essays, see Goldman (1981) and Woolf (2001).

interpreters instead focused on tensions between Wollstonecraft's emphasis on reason and the possibilities of romantic and sexual love (Kaplan 1986: 31–50; Gatens 1991). Initiating a new strand of interpretation, Barbara Taylor aims at reconciling Wollstonecraft's views on reason, God and erotic love by emphasizing Platonist elements in her thought, according to which 'the epistemic impulse toward Him is essentially imaginative and erotic in character' (Taylor 2003: 108). Most recently, scholars have been concerned with Wollstonecraft's concept of friendship, its importance for her views on ideal marriage (Abbey 1999; Taylor 2007: 145–62; Kendrick 2016) and politics (Sapiro 1992: 180–1; Frazer 2008), as well as its relations to Aristotle's concept of virtue friendship (Taylor 2007: 135–62; Kendrick 2016 and 2019).

Scholars have mainly focused on Wollstonecraft's views of either love or friendship. My aim in this section is to discuss the connections between the two. In Subsection 5.1, I give a brief overview of the eighteenth-century views that form the context of Wollstonecraft's work. Subsection 5.2 examines Wollstonecraft's discussions of love and friendship in relation to marriage, and Subsection 5.3 summarizes her conception of love and identifies some of its tensions.

5.1 The Eighteenth-Century Context

Many eighteenth-century authors agreed that the imagination plays a crucial role in romantic love. Rousseau, in his characteristically pessimistic vein, summarizes the romanticizing role of the imagination in *Emile*:

> And what is true love itself if it is not chimera, lie, and illusion? We love the image we make for ourselves far more than we love the object to which we apply it. If we saw what we love exactly as it is, there would be no more love on earth. When we stop loving, the person we love remains the same as before, but we no longer see her in the same way. The magic veil drops, and love disappears. (Rousseau 1979: 329)

The role of the imagination in friendship is less evident, but imagination particularly constitutes a basis for friendship in Scottish thinkers such as David Hume and Adam Smith.[31] By our imagination we may, as Smith writes, 'enter as it were into [the other person's] body, and become in some measure the same person with him' (Smith 2002: 12). Smith calls this human capacity 'sympathy' and as opposed to the subjective romantic imagination, it focuses on general human tendencies and conditions, such as the capacity to feel pain or the recognition of true virtue.

---

[31] Here I restrict my discussion to Smith's position, but I discuss Hume's view on love and friendship in Reuter (2005).

According to Smith, friendship is both one of 'the social and benevolent affections' (Smith 2002: 47) and an essential part of a virtuous character. When discussing friendship in terms of virtue, Smith distinguishes friendship, which he considers exclusively between men, from love between the sexes. Echoing Aristotle's discussion of friendship in the *Nicomachean Ethics* (VIII 3. 1156a6–1156b32), Smith singles out the highest form of friendship 'which is founded altogether upon esteem and appropriation of [the friend's] good conduct and behaviour, confirmed by much experience and long acquaintance' and which 'can exist only among men of virtue' (Smith 2002: 264). This attachment, which is 'founded on the love of virtue', is 'certainly, of all attachments, the most virtuous; so it is likewise the happiest, as well as the most permanent and secure' (Smith 2002: 264). Smith borrows Aristotle's description of virtue friendship in many of its details, but gives it his own foundation based on a distinction between different forms of sympathy. According to Smith, friendship between virtuous persons arises from 'a natural sympathy, from an involuntary feeling that the persons to whom we attach ourselves are the natural and proper objects of esteem and appropriation' (Smith 2002: 264). This 'natural sympathy' is distinguished from 'a sympathy which has been assumed and rendered habitual for the sake of conveniency and accommodation' and which forms the basis for friendships among family members, neighbours and colleagues (Smith 2002: 264). Smith concludes that friendships based on the love of virtue 'need not be confined to a single person, but may safely embrace all the wise and virtuous' (Smith 2002: 264). This further characterizes the universal nature of virtuous friendship.

It is important to note that according to Smith, the object of a true virtuous friendship actually has the virtuous characteristics we attribute to that person and is thus the proper object of the esteem we feel. This view is significantly different from Rousseau's picture of romantic love, where the characteristics we attribute to the beloved are the makings of our imagination. The character of truth-grounded – rather than wishful – esteem with long acquaintance guarantees the stable nature of virtuous friendship.

As we saw from the passage cited at the beginning of this section (Section 5), Wollstonecraft's characterization of friendship as 'founded on principle, and cemented by time' (*Works* 5: 142) resembles Smith's view, but with two important exceptions. First, whereas Smith refers to natural sympathy as the basis of virtuous friendship, Wollstonecraft refers to reason. This difference illustrates the distinction between Smith's moral sense theory and Wollstonecraft's emphasis on reason as the basis of virtue. Second, she seems to put more emphasis on the particular nature of friendships. She would not claim that a person can have only one friend, but Smith's conviction that all virtuous and wise people are our potential friends may be questioned on the same grounds as the Houyhnhnm friendship towards 'the whole Race' (Swift 2005: 250), discussed in Subsection 3.2.

Smith distinguishes friendship from romantic love, and he sees the role of imagination in love similarly to Rousseau. When arguing that friendship need not be limited to one single relation, Smith points out that those 'who would confine friendship to two persons, seem to confound the wise security of friendship with the jealousy and folly of love' (Smith 2002: 264). He categorizes love as a prime example of passions 'which take their origin from a particular turn or habit of the imagination'. These passions are 'perfectly natural ... but little sympathized with' (Smith 2002: 38). This is so because other people's imaginations have not taken the same particular turn towards the same person, therefore they cannot enter into the same feeling or eagerness of emotion. From other people's point of view, love is always 'in some measure, ridiculous' (Smith 2002: 38). Love is also characterized by the 'grossness of that passion, which mixes with, and is, perhaps, the foundation of love' (Smith 2002: 39). Like Rousseau, Smith thinks that love, as opposed to friendship, is 'entirely disproportioned to the value of the object' (Smith 2002: 38). This is why other people cannot perceive the value attributed by the lover.

Smith's love and friendship are structurally different above all because love is based on a particular turn of the imagination, which cannot arouse sympathy in others, whereas friendship is based on universalizing characteristics of sympathy. Wollstonecraft agrees on the idea that love is a particular turn of the imagination, but in her view, friendship is based on principles of reason, not on sympathy. Love and friendship are often opposites, according to Wollstonecraft, but, as we will see, she does account for cases where the two merge, when the object of love turns out to be the worthy object of friendship.

5.2 Love and Esteem

The views of Rousseau and Smith show that Wollstonecraft's opposition between love and friendship derives from her intellectual context. Her views are most interesting when she departs from this context. Smith discusses friendship exclusively between men, while Wollstonecraft is primarily interested in friendship between the sexes, arguing that friendship must constitute the basis for marriage. Her focus is often on the differences between the emotions of love and esteem. In *Rights of Woman*, she points out that 'Love, considered as an animal appetite, cannot long feed on itself without expiring. And this extinction in its own flame, may be termed the violent death of love' (*Works* 5: 141). As in her general discussions of the passions and the imagination, here Wollstonecraft is concerned about the problem of contentment. Animal appetites expire when they are gratified and lovers will soon 'endeavour to fill the void' with new objects of attention (*Works* 5: 142). Wollstonecraft contrasts love, considered as an animal appetite, with friendship based on esteem. She writes:

> Personal attachment is a very happy foundation for friendship; yet, when even two virtuous young people marry, it would, perhaps, be happy if some circumstances checked their passion; if the recollection of some prior attachment, or disappointed affection, made it on one side, at least, rather a match founded on esteem. In that case they would look beyond the present moment, and try to render the whole of life respectable, by forming a plan to regulate a friendship which only death ought to dissolve.
>
> (*Works* 5: 142)

According to this passage, mutual esteem constitutes a firmer foundation for matrimonial friendship than personal affection, such as love. Interestingly, Wollstonecraft holds that people who have experienced disappointed love are more inclined to esteem their partner in marriage. We may read the remark in the light of her view that though passions often lead one astray, in the long run they strengthen the capacity for judgement (see Subsection 3.1.2). When discussing John Gregory's influential conduct book *A Father's Legacy to His Daughters* (1774), Wollstonecraft criticizes the attempt to

> exclude pleasure and improvement, by vainly wishing to ward off sorrow and error – and by thus guarding the heart and mind, destroy also all their energy. – It is far better to be often deceived than never to trust; to be disappointed in love than never to love; to lose a husband's fondness than to forfeit his esteem. (*Works* 5: 170)

Wollstonecraft argues that girls and boys should be allowed to love, despite the fact that these romances may end in sorrow and even lead to the committing of errors.[32] This is not merely a question of youthful pleasure, but of improvement and of strengthening the energy of heart and mind. Esteem constitutes the most important basis for marriage here as well, but the wife has dared to trust and love and deserves her husband's esteem – even if she may lose his fondness, a much pettier emotion.

Wollstonecraft repeatedly emphasizes the opposite natures of love and esteem. She writes:

---

[32] In another passage, Wollstonecraft goes as far as defending unwed mothers (*Works* 5: 140).

In order to admire or esteem any thing for a continuance, we must, at least, have our curiosity excited by knowing, in some degree, what we admire; for we are unable to estimate the value of qualities and virtues above our comprehension. Such a respect, when it is felt, may be very sublime; ... but human love must have grosser ingredients ....

Love is, in a great degree, an arbitrary passion, and will reign, like some other stalking mischiefs, by its own authority, without deigning to reason; and it may also be easily distinguished from esteem, the foundation of friendship, because it is often excited by evanescent beauties and graces, though, to give an energy to the sentiment, something more solid must deepen their impressions and set the imagination to work, to make the most fair – the first good. (*Works* 5: 188)

Wollstonecraft makes several claims in these passages. First, justified esteem requires knowledge of virtue. Second, though esteem is in itself sublime, it is not sufficient for love, which requires 'grosser ingredients'. Wollstonecraft's expression echoes Smith's claim that the 'grossness of that passion' mixes with and 'is, perhaps, the foundation of love' (Smith 2002: 39). Third, love is arbitrary and cannot be easily guided by reason. Fourth, love excited merely by beauties and grace remains fleeting and is in need of more solid ingredients, such as – we may assume – virtue. Finally, imagination is required to make the object of love the first good. Wollstonecraft indicates that esteem lacks the ardour of love and love lacks the solidity of esteem. Though she thinks that the two emotions are essentially different in character, under ideal circumstances they can be brought together. Some paragraphs later, she continues: 'Supposing, however, for a moment, that women were, in some future revolution of time, to become what I sincerely wish them to be, even love would acquire more serious dignity, and be purified in its own fires; and virtue giving true delicacy to their affections, they would turn with disgust from a rake' (*Works* 5: 188–9).

The opposition between love and esteem is at least in part due to the fact that custom and lack of education incline both women and men to love for the wrong reasons. When women and men learn to esteem virtue, they become inclined to love with dignity and women can avoid being deceived by rakes. In this passage love is not extinguished 'in its own flame' and condemned to violent death, as in the description of love considered as an animal appetite (*Works* 5: 141), but rather 'purified in its own fires' (*Works* 5: 189). The purification means that superficial physical delicacy is replaced by the true delicacy of virtue. Most importantly, love is not replaced by esteem, but rather transformed into a dignified form of love. This means that love does not lose its ardour; instead, that ardour finds a solid basis. Love achieves the same dual character of affection and virtue, which makes friendship one of 'the fairest virtues' (*Works* 5: 23).

Wollstonecraft articulates one of her most empathetic descriptions of how love can purify itself in a letter to Imlay. This personal love letter contains a strong element of persuasion, but it articulates a philosophical position, which makes it an interesting addition to Wollstonecraft's published writings. She writes:

> The common run of men, I know, with strong health and gross appetite, must have variety to banish *ennui*, because the imagination never lends its magic wand to convert appetite into love, cemented by according reason. Ah! my friend, you know not the ineffable delight, the exquisite pleasure, which arises from a unison of affection and desire, when the whole soul and senses are abandoned to a lively imagination, that renders every emotion delicate and rapturous. Yes; these are emotions over which satiety has no power, and the recollection of which, even disappointment cannot disenchant; but they do not exist without self-denial. These emotions, more or less strong, appear to me to be the distinctive characteristic of genius, ... I consider those minds as the most strong and original, whose imagination acts as the stimulus to their senses. (*Letters*: 297)

In this passage, the main attempt is to convert appetite into love rather than love into friendship, but love is to be 'cemented by according reason' and in this respect resembles friendship. As in the description of loving with dignity (*Works* 5: 189), love is acquiring the nature of a virtue, which requires that one give up mere self-interest; but contrary to most of Wollstonecraft's other writings, the letter to Imlay makes it clear that sexual desire is not supposed to be left behind, but rather to be purified, focused on one person and upheld by the imagination. It is the task of the imagination to 'enlarge the object, and make it the most desirable', as Wollstonecraft writes in *Rights of Woman* (*Works* 5: 127).

In *Rights of Woman*, Wollstonecraft argues that in order for a marriage to last, love must 'subside into friendship'. She writes:

> Were women more rationally educated, could they take a more comprehensive view of things, they would be contented to love but once in their lives; and after marriage calmly let passion subside into friendship – into that tender intimacy, which is the best refuge from care; yet is built on such pure, still affections, that idle jealousies would not be allowed to disturb the discharge of the sober duties of life, or to engross the thoughts that ought to be otherwise employed. (*Works* 5: 189)

The tone of this calm description differs markedly from Wollstonecraft's passionate letter to Imlay, but in order to grasp how profound the differences are, we need to ask what is implied by the 'tender intimacy' of marriage. In one particular passage in *Rights of Woman*, Wollstonecraft describes the intimacy between spouses in a way that does indicate a lasting sexual relationship. She writes:

> A man, or a woman, of any feeling, must always wish to convince a beloved object that it is the caresses of the individual, not the sex, that are received and returned with pleasure; and that the heart, rather than the senses, is moved. Without this natural delicacy, love becomes a selfish personal gratification that soon degrades the character. (*Works* 5: 169)

This passage resembles Wollstonecraft's letter to Imlay in several interesting ways. In both passages, we find that a general appetite for the opposite sex and the gratification of the senses are opposed to an individualized desire for a particular human being and a gratification of the heart. Mere animal-like appetite is selfish and degrading, whereas the unison of affection and desire for an individual being is worthy of a virtuous person and even a genius. Wollstonecraft seems to think that love may either degenerate into mere appetite or develop into a principled affection, which, like friendship, becomes a virtue. When discussing the education of young people, we even find her referring to love and friendship in tandem, cemented by equality. She writes: 'I presuppose, that such a degree of equality should be established between the sexes as would shut out gallantry and coquetry, yet allow friendship and love to temper the heart for the discharge of higher duties' (*Works* 5: 241).

In these passages, the problem is not so much the sexual element of love as such, but the 'idle jealousies', which so easily intertwine with love and desire. What happens when 'passion subside[s] into friendship' is not that the married couple stop loving each other or give up their sexual desires, but rather that they create an atmosphere of 'tender intimacy' and justified trust, which does not leave space for jealousy. Interestingly, we may interpret Wollstonecraft's emphasis on 'the caresses of the individual' as a kind of remedy against jealousy, which convinces the loved one of her or his uniqueness.

5.3 Wollstonecraft's Conception of Love

Still, there are passages where Wollstonecraft seems to challenge the picture I have just drawn. Most important is the passage cited at the beginning of Subsection 5.2, where she questions the role of personal attachment as a basis for marriage and recommends marriages where 'the recollection of some prior attachment . . . made it on one side, at least, rather a match founded on esteem' (*Works* 5: 142). Wollstonecraft seems to vacillate between the idea that marriage is a friendship built purely on esteem and the idea of dignified love subsiding into friendship. In all cases, it is better 'to be disappointed in love than never to love' (*Works* 5: 170), but in the first case disappointed love is succeeded by esteem for another person and in the second case love is not disappointed, but subsides into friendship. Wollstonecraft's hesitation seems to be partly about human abilities and partly about the compatibility of love and friendship as concepts and emotions. She did write that in 'a great degree, love and friendship cannot subsist in the same bosom' (*Works* 5: 142). We can distinguish four separate problems here, which I will discuss one by one.

The first problem is whether humans are able to become sufficiently virtuous in order to love with dignity and accept the self-denial required for focusing one's desire on a single individual. Here Wollstonecraft seems to waver between her optimistic view on the potential of education and her pessimistic view on the destructive effects of social realities. She is never really a pessimist concerning human nature, since that would contradict her belief in perfectibility, but most humans are weak creatures and easily corrupted by their circumstances. These circumstances include the unequal relations between women and men, which make all kinds of friendships between the sexes difficult to achieve. Human weakness can also be seen as the origin of jealousy, which may arise from a lack of trust or trustworthiness. In *Rights of Men*, Wollstonecraft emphasizes that 'the basis of friendship is mutual respect, and not a commercial treaty' (*Work* 5: 39). As long as marriage is based on an idea of ownership, it will be riddled with jealousy.

The second problem concerns whether love and friendship contain conceptual features that are incompatible. When looking at the concepts of love, friendship and esteem, we find Wollstonecraft struggling with received meanings that she in part adopts and in part attempts to redefine. In accordance with Edmund Burke's distinction between the sublime and the beautiful, she relates esteem to the former and love to the latter concept (see also Subsection 3.2). When discussing the love of God in *Rights of Men*, Wollstonecraft explicitly criticizes Burke's conception of women's 'beautiful weakness', which is intended to 'inspire love' (*Works* 5: 46). She argues that if one accepts Burke's claim 'that respect and love are antagonist principles' our love of God's perfections become inconceivable (*Works* 5: 46). Wollstonecraft also criticizes the idea that love is essentially love of delicacy and weakness in *Rights of Woman* (e.g. *Works* 5: 116), but as we have seen, in exploring the differing natures of love and esteem (or respect) she takes up the idea that these are antagonistic principles. Her hesitations on the relations between love, esteem and friendship in marriage partly reflect the tension between her attempt to criticize Burke's influential account and her own reliance on the received understanding of these concepts.

The third philosophically important problem concerns the relation between universality and individuality. As we saw in Subsection 5.1, Smith contrasts 'the wise security of friendship' with 'the jealousy and folly of love' (Smith 2002: 264). He distinguishes the universal character of friendship, built on 'esteem and appropriation' (Smith 2002: 264), from the individualized character of love, based on a particular turn of the imagination (Smith 2002: 38). Smith relates jealousy to the particularized and unstable character of love and states it cannot disturb friendship, since friendship is universal and not limited to one particular individual. Wollstonecraft adopts a similar distinction between the characteristics of friendship and love, but the very context of her discussions of friendship – marriage – rules out Smith's idea that friendship can embrace all wise and virtuous individuals. Marriage is by definition an individual relation between two human beings. In order to make mutual esteem the basis of marriage, Wollstonecraft has to combine esteem felt for the virtuous in general with individualized affection, where the imagination labours to 'enlarge the object, and make it the most desirable' (*Works* 5: 127). Since Wollstonecraft is not drawing Smith's conceptual line between universal friendship and individual love, she needs to emphasize the stable nature of friendship and its 'tender intimacy' in order to fend off jealousy (*Works* 5: 189). From her point of view, part of the challenge in a happy marriage is to achieve the stability of friendship without losing the particularity of a love relationship. Far from describing marriage as a relation of general esteem, Wollstonecraft describes an intimate relationship, which she distinguishes from a general appetite for the opposite sex as well as from general esteem for all the wise and virtuous. A marriage of the latter kind would resemble the marriages of the Houyhnhnm, satirized by Swift and critically perceived by Wollstonecraft (see Subsection 3.2).

The fourth problem is also of the utmost philosophical importance and concerns the value of the beloved person. Like Rousseau and Smith, Wollstonecraft thinks that love is based on a particular turn of the imagination. She shares their worry about the often deceptive character of romantic love, but she does not seem to think that love is necessarily 'disproportioned to the value of the object' (Smith 2002: 38). As we have seen, when love acquires 'serious dignity' and 'true delicacy' through virtue, women do not fall in love with rakes, but choose virtuous partners, who are worthy objects of their affections (*Works* 5: 189). The imagination makes the object in question 'the most desirable' (*Works* 5: 127), but does not necessarily misrepresent the value of the object. Objects of love may turn out to be worthy objects of the lover's esteem and in these cases, love develops into friendship. How exactly should we understand Wollstonecraft's view on the value of the beloved?

In recent philosophical discussions on the nature of love, we find a distinction between views that love is an appraisal of the value of its object and views that love is a bestowal of value on the beloved.[33] In both views, the value of the beloved is in some respect real – it is either pre-existing in the object or given to the object. Yet, whereas the appraisal view relies on criteria for justification (such as the beloved being particularly virtuous), the bestowal view does not easily allow for justification. Wollstonecraft's (and Smith's) characterizations of friendship and its reliance on esteem are typical of an appraisal view: friendship and esteem can be justified by reference to the virtuous character of the friend. Wollstonecraft's (and Smith's and Rousseau's) view of love, however, is typical of the bestowal view, where the imagination is the bestower. Wollstonecraft's attempt to combine love and friendship can be characterized as an effort to seek an intermediate position between the appraisal and bestowal views by combining elements from both (compare Helm 2021: 23–5). When telling Imlay that the imagination should lend 'its magic wand to convert appetite into love, cemented by according reason' (*Letters*: 297) she is stating that the imagination bestows love in accordance with reasoned appraisal of the beloved's value. Wollstonecraft had to struggle with tensions arising from the objective characteristics of appraisal and the subjective characteristics of bestowal, but she avoids the dichotomous nature of Smith's account, according to which all the wise and virtuous are equally eligible to claim our friendship, whereas love is necessarily disproportionate and unjustifiable.

6 Knowledge

The question of knowledge plays a fundamental role in Wollstonecraft's moral philosophy, but she does not develop a systematic epistemology. She was aware of the ongoing epistemological debates of her time, though, and in one of the few existing scholarly discussions of her epistemological views, Isabelle Bour points out that Wollstonecraft's works 'evince a testing of, and sometimes tensions between, various epistemological models' (Bour 2019: 311). The most important tension is between the doctrine of innate ideas defended by Richard Price and the various forms of empiricism that dominated Wollstonecraft's intellectual environment.

The question of knowledge is also crucial to Wollstonecraft's feminism. She addresses knowledge explicitly in her criticism of Rousseau's defence of gendered social roles, which I discuss in Subsection 6.1. In Subsection 6.2, I examine the tension between innate elements and empiricist features in Wollstonecraft's epistemological thought.

---

[33] For an excellent overview of the discussion, see Helm (2021) and the references given there.

6.1 Criticism of Gendered Knowledge

Wollstonecraft argues that women as well as men must be 'allowed to found their virtue on knowledge' (*Works* 5: 245). The close connection between virtue and knowledge is part of her criticism of relativist views, which conflate true morality with culturally relative manners. This criticism constitutes the backbone of her feminism. In *Rights of Woman*, she writes that: 'For man and woman, truth, if I understand the meaning of the word, must be the same; yet the fanciful female character, so prettily drawn by poets and novelists, demanding the sacrifice of truth and sincerity, virtue becomes a relative idea' (*Works* 5: 120).

Wollstonecraft argues that truth cannot depend on gender: 'truth, as it is a simple principle, which admits of no modification, would be common to both [genders]' (*Works* 5: 105). If virtue is to be based on truth, it requires knowledge of truth, and Wollstonecraft insists 'that not only the virtue, but the *knowledge* of the two sexes should be the same in nature, if not in degree' (*Works* 5: 108). Depending on their education and social circumstances, women and men may possess different degrees of knowledge, but regardless of who holds it, the nature of knowledge is the same. Wollstonecraft is not consciously developing a criticism of ad hominem arguments,[34] but her emphasis on the ungendered nature of knowledge has the consequence that the characteristics of the knower do not affect the qualities of knowledge.

Wollstonecraft embarks on a criticism of gendered knowledge, which culminates in a criticism of Rousseau's concept of knowledge. Her discussion is accompanied by a long footnote, where she cites his discussion of gendered knowledge in William Kendrick's eighteenth-century translation of *Emile*. Rousseau argues that 'researches into abstract and speculative truths, the principles and axioms of sciences, in short, every thing which tends to generalize our ideas, is not the proper province of women' (Rousseau 1763: 74; cf. Rousseau 1979: 387). Instead, women should 'make observations, which direct men to the establishment of general principles' and 'apply those principles which men have discovered' (Rousseau 1763: 74). In short: 'women observe, men reason' (Rousseau 1763: 75). This is indeed the education of 'half beings' (*Works* 5: 108). Rousseau's description is in principle egalitarian in the sense that the roles of women and men are different, but complementary and equally necessary. Still, when read by an audience that considers abstract truths and generalized ideas to be the goal of knowledge seeking, the description does

---

[34] She does indeed occasionally use ad hominem arguments herself, as when she claims that Rousseau's conception of the relation between the sexes 'could only have occurred to a man, whose imagination had been allowed to run wild, and refine on the impressions made by exquisite senses; ... which gratifies the pride and libertinism of man' (*Works* 5: 109).

make women mere helpmates. Wollstonecraft is very clear on her understanding of the nature of true knowledge:

> The power of generalizing ideas, of drawing comprehensive conclusions from individual observations, is the only acquirement, for an immortal being, that really deserves the name of knowledge. Merely to observe, without endeavouring to account for any thing, may (in a very incomplete manner) serve as the common sense of life; but where is the store laid up that is to clothe the soul when it leaves the body? (*Works* 5: 123)

As we saw in Subsection 2.3, Wollstonecraft identifies 'the power of generalizing' with reason. When Rousseau denies women the ability to generalize, he is, from her perspective, simultaneously denying that they are reasoning creatures.

Rousseau's description of women who observe and men who generalize, like Wollstonecraft's critique of it, is based on a predominantly empiricist picture of knowledge acquisition. Knowledge requires observation as well as generalization and abstraction. In her criticism of Rousseau, Wollstonecraft denigrates the role of observation, which merely serves 'the common sense of life', but she is well aware that the very activity of generalizing ideas requires 'individual observations'. Wollstonecraft's empiricist approach is strengthened by her emphasis on the necessity of experience (Subsection 3.1.2), which exercises the human faculties and gives 'many new ideas' (*Works* 5: 16). Her remarks indicate an empiricist conception of some form of sense-based primary ideas, which form the basis for generalization and abstraction. Nevertheless, Wollstonecraft refers to the immortal nature of generalized ideas, which 'clothe the soul when it leaves the body' (*Works* 5: 123). Here she indicates that general ideas are real existing things, not mere abstractions. These ideas belong to the soul and follow it into the afterlife. This conception shows affinity with Price's Platonist understanding of universal innate ideas rather than with a pure empiricism.

6.2 Innate Capacities and Empiricist Features

Natalie Taylor has indeed argued that Wollstonecraft defends the view that 'principles of truth are innate' (Taylor 2007: 102). She interprets Wollstonecraft's position as contrary to Locke's empiricism. As textual evidence, Taylor refers to Wollstonecraft's early work on education, *Thoughts on the Education of Daughters* (1787). Here Wollstonecraft writes: 'It is, in my opinion, a well-proved fact, that principles of truth are innate. Without reasoning we assent to many truths; we feel their force, and artful sophistry can only blunt those feelings which nature has implanted in us as instinctive guards to virtue' (*Works* 4: 9). If we emphasize the first sentence and interpret 'reasoning' as mere deduction separated from the intuitions of reason, Wollstonecraft's claim resembles Richard Price's doctrine of intuitively perceived innate truths (see Subsection 2.3). If we instead emphasize the latter part of the passage and the reference to the 'feelings which nature has implanted in us as instinctive guards to virtue', she seems to have moral sense theory in mind rather than Price's rationalism. Most moral sense theorists (see Subsection 4.1) did consider moral sense innate to human beings, but this is a different form of innatism from the rationalist doctrine of innate principles and ideas, which Taylor wants to attribute to Wollstonecraft. Taylor searches *Rights of Woman* for additional textual evidence (2007: 103–5). She notes two passages where Wollstonecraft refers to God, who has 'impressed them [utopian dreams] on my soul' (*Works* 5: 105) and 'stamped [the soul] with the heavenly image' (*Works* 5: 122).

Wollstonecraft thinks that humans are 'stamped' with the innate capacity for reason. This is a result of humans being created in the image of God. The capacity for reason enables humans to know universal principles, but in the context of *Rights of Woman*, it is not evident that Wollstonecraft thinks that we have innate knowledge of these principles. On the contrary, she seems to argue that humans know universal principles through the activities of generalization and abstraction. Taylor concludes that for Wollstonecraft 'the notion that "every being may become virtuous by the exercise of its own reason" is an innate principle' (Taylor 2007: 104). Here Taylor seems to confuse innate and universal principles. Wollstonecraft agrees that it is universally true that humans may only become virtuous by exercising their own reason. The claim is a universal and immutable principle, but it is not innate; that is, it cannot be known independently of experience. As we saw in Subsection 3.1.2, exercising reason is itself dependent on experience, and humans know principles only by generalizing from experience.

It is useful to compare Wollstonecraft's position with Catharine Macaulay's criticism of innate principles. In *Letters on Education*, Macaulay writes that: '[R]eason is always able to discern the moral difference of things, whenever they are fairly and plainly proposed; which, as I take it, establishes an immutable and abstract fitness in a more satisfactory manner than what is called a moral consciousness from innate principles' (Macaulay 1996: 193–4): she holds that 'Morals must be taught on immutable Principles' (Macaulay 1996: 198), but these principles are not innately given. In her review of *Letters on Education*, Wollstonecraft refers approvingly to Macaulay's conception of immutability and to her conclusion that 'true wisdom ... is as useful to women as to men' (Macaulay 1996: 201; *Works* 7: 314). Scholars agree that reading and reviewing Macaulay's book made Wollstonecraft increasingly aware of the problems involved in gendered education and strengthened her conviction that girls and boys must be taught according to the same principles (e.g. Gunther-Canada 2003). Macaulay may also have affected Wollstonecraft's understanding of the relation between immutable principles and experience.

Macaulay's epistemological position is explicitly empiricist. She emphasizes that experience 'is the only efficacious instructor of man. It is by an extensive knowledge of the relation of things, and the effects of causes, by which our reason becomes a more valuable gift than those instinctive powers which nature has bestowed on the brute' (Macaulay 1996: 23). She uses the empiricist criticism of 'the doctrine of innate ideas' in order to argue that there are no 'natural qualities of the female mind' (Macaulay 1996: 203). If the human mind is a *tabula rasa* at birth, then specific female and male modes of thought and action must be characteristics acquired through experience. Macaulay explicates her empiricism in her discussions of the association of ideas. Karen Green has argued that in *Letters on Education*, Macaulay 'accepted the importance of the "power of association"', which had been 'refined and extended by David Hartley' (Green 2020: 180). Hartley's doctrine of association formed the basis for his doctrine of necessity (Greenberg 2013: 255; also Subsection 2.2), and Macaulay makes similar remarks on association. She emphasizes that 'the human mind . . . is quite passive in receiving impressions' and these impressions do easily 'lead into the train of their associates' (Macaulay 1996: 163; 149–50). The power of association makes the education of children particularly challenging and here Macaulay quotes Rousseau to argue that one must reduce 'the first part of education to a system merely negative' (Macaulay 1996: 126). The education of children younger than twelve, the age by which he assumes reason has developed, must first and foremost be 'negative' in the sense that it prevents harmful impressions, which lead into malevolent trains of association. In *Emile*, Rousseau writes that 'the first education ought to be purely negative. It consists not at all in teaching virtue of truth but in securing the heart from vice and the mind from error' (Rousseau 1979: 93; see also Subsection 3.1.2).

Like Locke, Macaulay is keen on combining her empiricist epistemology with the immutability of moral principles. The problem is aptly summarized by Green: 'if we acquire ideas through the senses, then it appears that there will have to be physical instantiations of these ideas, in order for us to acquire them' (Green 2020: 155). How can we know the existence and nature of abstract moral principles? Macaulay addresses the question in a Lockean framework. Her argument in *Letters on Education* (Macaulay 1996: 347–8) summarizes a more detailed discussion in her earlier book *A Treatise on the Immutability of Moral Truth* (1783). There she asks 'whether there could have been such a moral entity as the abstract notion which we frame of justice' even if God had not created rational beings who may stand in just relations to each other. If moral principles are immutable, we must assume that they exist independently of particular created beings. Macaulay continues by responding to her own question:

> To which we answer, that, according to Mr Locke's observations on the power of the mind in framing abstract ideas, complete ideas of this kind [i.e. justice] may be framed, if there were no archtypes [*sic*] in nature corresponding to them. If, says he, an idea could have been framed of homicide, the same as we have now of it, the idea would have been just, though no homicide had ever been committed; so, the nature, complexion, and reality of justice and injustice, would always have been the same, if the Almighty had never brought into existence any rational beings, whose mutual relation required the exercise and operation of this moral rule.
>
> (Macaulay Graham 1783: 38–9)

It is not clear exactly what passage from Locke's works Macaulay has in mind,[35] but she is right in thinking he attempts to show that morality is immutable and can be known regardless of whether we have experience of particular moral relations. Locke compares morality with mathematics: '*Morality is capable of Demonstration*, as well as Mathematicks: Since the precise real Essence of the Things moral Words stand for, may be perfectly known; and so the Congruity, or Incongruity of the Things themselves, be certainly discovered, in which consists perfect Knowledge' (*Essay Concerning Human Understanding* book III, chapter XI, § 16; Locke 1975: 516).

Locke's position was widely debated in the eighteenth century (Stanton 2013: 26–33) and Richard Price famously challenged the very idea that mathematics can be demonstrated on a purely empiricist basis. Still, for authors such as Macaulay and at least to some extent Wollstonecraft, who wanted to combine the immutability of morality with a criticism of innate ideas, Locke did make an attempt in the right direction and provide a philosophical authority to refer to.

In *Rights of Woman*, written soon after having read and reviewed Macaulay's *Letters on Education*, Wollstonecraft has abandoned the language of innate principles. She even makes fun of the idea that 'in a pre-existent state the soul

---

[35] The most likely passages are those in *Essay Concerning Human Understanding* book III, chapter V, where Locke discusses names of mixed modes and relations using morally relevant ideas as examples. He argues that the truth of the idea of adultery or incest does not depend on whether anyone has witnessed such acts; instead 'it suffices here, that Men have put together ... one complex *Idea*, that makes the *Archetype*, and specifick *Idea*, whether ever any such Action were committed *in rerum natura*, or no' (Locke 1975: 429). Some paragraphs later Locke mentions murder as a similar example (Locke 1975: 430). Macaulay seems to restrict her use of archetype to what is instantiated in nature, whereas Locke does not, but most importantly, neither author uses archetype as a synonym for an innate idea.

was fond of dress, and brought this inclination with it into a new body' as an explanation of why girls are more occupied with dress than boys (*Works* 5: 97). Here Wollstonecraft, as Macaulay, relies on the criticism of innate ideas in order to argue against innate gendered abilities. *Rights of Woman* also includes a chapter focusing explicitly on the 'determinate effect an early association of ideas has on the character' (*Works* 5: 185). As pointed out by Isabelle Bour, Wollstonecraft's account of association may have been influenced by Hartley,[36] but it is important to note that she resists a thoroughly deterministic account of association. Wollstonecraft distinguishes between habitual and instantaneous association. Whereas the capacity for instantaneous association is characteristic of natural geniuses, described as 'the glowing minds that concentrate pictures for their fellow-creatures', the 'generality of people' are only affected by habitual association (*Works* 5: 186). Such habitual association is that which has 'a great effect on the moral character of mankind; and by which a turn is given to the mind that commonly remains throughout life' (*Works* 5: 186). Here Wollstonecraft agrees with Macaulay and Rousseau, and emphasizes that habitual associations, which have established themselves in childhood, can 'seldom be disentangled by reason' (*Works* 5: 186). Still, as we saw in Subsection 3.1.2, she agrees with Locke rather than Rousseau on the question of reasoning with children. When discussing habitual association of ideas, she argues that the 'habitual slavery, to first impressions, has a more baneful effect on the female than the male character, because ... dry employments of the understanding, tend to deaden the feelings and break associations that do violence to reason' (*Works* 5: 186). Boys, with whom parents and tutors reason from an early age, are less inclined to become slaves to malevolent habitual associations than girls are.

There is insufficient textual evidence to show that Wollstonecraft holds an epistemology based on innate principles and ideas, but neither is she a systematic empiricist. There is no denying that she often uses Platonizing language, referring to knowledge that 'clothe[s] the soul' (*Works* 5: 123) and to a divine maker, who 'impress[es]' or 'stamp[s]' the soul (*Works* 5: 105, 122). It is most likely that Wollstonecraft received her influences of philosophical Platonism from Richard Price. In *Principal Questions and Difficulties in Morals*, Price develops an explicit criticism of Locke's and Hume's empiricisms (Price 1758: 63). He is interested in the origin of moral ideas and argues that all ideas cannot be derived purely by sensation and reflection (Price 1758: 18). Price is using a classical Platonist argument to claim that the empiricist notion of reflection actually assumes the general idea that it claims to find. He writes:

---

[36] Bour refers to the contextual fact that Joseph Priestley's abridgement of *Hartley's Theory of the Human Mind, on the Principle of the Association of Ideas* was published by Joseph Johnson in 1775 and reissued in 1790 (Bour 2019: 317).

'Thus from any particular idea of a triangle, it is said, we can frame the general one; but does not the very reflexion said to be necessary to this, on a greater or lesser triangle, clearly imply, that the general idea is already in the mind?' (Price 1758: 42). Price argues that the mind would not be able to compare lesser and greater triangles if it did not innately identify them as triangles. He is not denying that when humans learn mathematics, they rely on sense perception as well as the intellect, which reflects on perceptions, but he argues that 'though not first in time', the understanding is 'the most fruitful and important source of our ideas' (Price 1758: 51). Here Price seems to make a distinction between ontological and temporal primacy, arguing that the idea of a triangle (for example) exists in the understanding prior to our reflections on particular triangles, even if the temporal process of learning proceeds from the particular towards the general.

This feature of Price's doctrine helps us understand Wollstonecraft's combination of a strongly empiricist language of generalization and abstraction with some Platonist elements. Throughout her writings, she is mostly interested in the temporal process of learning or attaining knowledge and she refers to this as a process of generalization. She does not discuss whether generalization is based only on the capacity for reflection, as Locke claims, or whether it is ontologically dependent on innate general ideas, as Price claims. She may well agree with Macaulay, who points out that it 'is perhaps the nature of all finite things to know only by comparison' (Macaulay 1996: 8).

In her review of Macaulay's *Letters on Education*, Wollstonecraft pointed out that the relation between the understanding and the will is 'a question, which metaphysicians have not yet brought to an issue' (*Works* 7: 321; see Subsection 2.2). It is plausible that she was similarly inclined not to take a definitive stand on the question of innate ideas. Her positions are in many respects very close to Macaulay's, but whereas Macaulay takes clear standpoints on several metaphysical issues, including questions of the will and of innate principles, Wollstonecraft tends to leave these questions without straightforward metaphysical answers. Rather than accusing Wollstonecraft of philosophical sloppiness, we can view her reluctance as a well-grounded awareness of the philosophical problems involved in the relation between the will and the understanding as well as between experience and innate capacities. From Wollstonecraft's point of view, the aim of philosophy is not metaphysical speculation, but rather to guide humans in their attempts to live virtuous lives.

7 Virtue

According to Wollstonecraft, virtue must be founded on truth or otherwise it will become 'a relative idea' of which 'men pretend arbitrarily to judge'

(*Works* 5: 120). As we saw in the previous section (Section 6), Wollstonecraft closely connects virtue and knowledge. Becoming virtuous requires adequate knowledge of truth. In this section, I examine Wollstonecraft's moral realism from the point of view of virtue. In Subsection 7.1, I cover Macaulay's concept of immutability and Price's views on the unity of virtue. In Subsection 7.2, I examine the connections Wollstonecraft makes between virtue and liberty, and in Subsection 7.3, her understanding of the unity of virtue, including her criticism of Rousseau's views on gendered virtue. In Subsection 7.4, I focus on the role of embodiment and summarize Wollstonecraft's interest in modesty as a non-gendered virtue. Scholars have labelled Wollstonecraft's concept of virtue Aristotelian as well as Platonist and in Subsection 7.5, I evaluate these interpretations. Finally, in Subsection 7.6 I discuss the role of duties and their relation to virtue.

7.1 Moral Realism

With Richard Price and Catharine Macaulay, Wollstonecraft belongs to a school of British moral realists who argue against what they judge to be the arbitrary nature of a morality based on either moral sentiments or utility. Macaulay addresses 'that famous sceptic, Mr Hume' (Macaulay 1996: 391) and criticizes the 'inconsistency and mutability' that 'hang on every system of morals founded on human sentiment' (Macaulay 1996: 193). Like Wollstonecraft, Macaulay connects mutability and 'the plea of utility' (Macaulay 1996: 193), which 'men pretend arbitrarily to judge' (*Works* 5: 120). Macaulay contrasts the arbitrary and mutable utility of men with the divine 'general utility' of the created order as a whole (Macaulay 1996: 193). She argues that '[m]orals must be thought on immutable Principles' (Macaulay 1996: 198) and holds that these principles must not only be the same for women and men, but must also regulate the virtues of the two sexes in the same way.[37] She argues against Rousseau that morality knows no 'sexual difference in character' (Macaulay 1996: 205). Macaulay scolds Rousseau for having 'made up a moral person of the union of the two sexes' and claims that 'for contradiction and absurdity' this view 'outdoes every metaphysical riddle that was ever formed in the schools' (Macaulay 1996: 206). As we will see in Subsection 7.3, Wollstonecraft builds her argument for the unity of virtue on a similar, but expanded, criticism of the idea that the union of the sexes may constitute a moral agent.

---

[37] Macaulay thus rules out immutable principles that would be the same for men and women but that would regulate their agency differently, such as an immutable principle stating that women must obey men.

In *Review of the Principal Questions and Difficulties in Morals*, Price develops a detailed philosophical criticism of moral sense theory, with a focus on Hutcheson's analogy between taste and moral sense. As we saw in Subsection 4.1, Price argues that morality is 'a thing equally steady, independent, and unchangeable with *all truth*' (Price 1758: 15). His aim is to show that moral qualities are real qualities existing in objects (also Perinetti 2013: 350). When discussing the nature of virtue, Price emphasizes its unity: with reference to Plato's *Meno* he writes that 'Virtue ... is necessarily one thing' (Price 1758: 287). Price enumerates separate virtues, but argues that 'from the very notion of them as *heads of virtue*, it is plain, that they all run up to one general idea, and should be considered as only different modifications' (Price 1758: 287). He aims to show 'how defective and how inconsistent a thing what we call *partial virtue* is' and continues: 'The same law that requires piety, requires benevolence, requires veracity, temperance, justice, gratitude, *etc.* All these rest on the same foundation, and are alike our indispensable duty' (Price 1758: 287–8).

Price's list of virtues is interesting not least because it brings together theological, moral, epistemological and political virtues into one uniform set of indispensable duty. The quote shows Price's emphasis on the moral law and on our duty to conform to this law. It is important to note that he considers the deontological emphasis on obligation to be a feature of the very idea of virtue. It is, according to Price, absurd to ask 'what *obliges* us to practise virtue?' (Price 1758: 191) since the obligatory nature belongs to virtue itself (see also Perinetti 2013: 351). Price combines these deontological features with a traditional virtue ethicist's emphasis on character. From the perspective of character, the unity of virtue is summarized as follows: 'True and genuine virtue must be uniform and universal. Nothing short of an *entire* good character can avail' (Price 1758: 288). Finally, we must note that though Price emphasizes the universal and unitary character of virtue, he is very aware of the particularity of circumstances. He writes:

> And as there is an endless variety of cases, and the situations of cases, and the situations of agents and things are ever changing; the universal law of rectitude, though in the abstract idea of it always invariably the same, must be continually varying, in the *external* observance of it, or in its aspect on particular effects and agents. (Price 1758: 286–7)

Turning now to Wollstonecraft's understanding of the nature of virtue, it is apparent that she sees the variety of circumstances, described by Price, as one reason why one can be truly virtuous only by the use of one's own reason.

Towards the end of *Rights of Woman*, when discussing the intellectual require-
ments of motherhood, Wollstonecraft combines the idea of the unity of virtue
and the fact of changing circumstances in a manner that has much in common
with Price's view. Wollstonecraft writes:

> The weakness of the mother will be visited on the children! And whilst
> women are educated to rely on their husbands for judgment, this must ever
> be the consequence, for there is no improving an understanding by halves, nor
> can any being act wisely from imitation, because in every circumstance of life
> there is a kind of individuality, which requires an exertion of judgment to
> modify general rules. The being who can think justly in one track, will soon
> extend its intellectual empire; and she who has sufficient judgment to manage
> her children, will not submit, right or wrong, to her husband, or patiently to
> the social laws which make a nonentity of a wife. (*Works* 5: 249)

The passage summarizes several aspects of Wollstonecraft's concept of virtue,
including her view on the relation between virtue and political change.

7.2 Liberty and Equality

In the passage cited at the end of Subsection 7.1, Wollstonecraft emphasizes that
women must be able to improve their understandings if they are to be good
mothers. Simultaneously, their improved understanding serves as a platform for
political change by making them mentally independent of both their husbands
and prejudiced social expectations. Mental independence is, according to
Wollstonecraft, necessary, but not sufficient in order to achieve social, financial
and political independence.[38]

The claim that dependence and obedience destroy virtue is a recurring theme
in Wollstonecraft's works. In *Rights of Woman*, she points out that 'the mind,
naturally weakened by depending on authority, never exerts its own powers, and
the obedient wife is thus rendered a weak indolent mother' (*Works* 5: 141). To
put it the other way around, virtue requires liberty (also Coffee 2016: 187–92).
Wollstonecraft first develops this idea in *Rights of Men*, when defending Price
against Burke's attack (see also Subsection 2.2). Here she discusses the possibility of a society built on virtue and writes that such 'a glorious change can only
be produced by liberty. Inequality of rank must ever impede the growth of
virtue, by vitiating the mind that submits or domineers' (*Works* 5: 46). It is
important to note that here domination and the lack of liberty impede virtue not

---

[38] Arguing against Rousseau's superficial ideal of female beauty, Wollstonecraft insists that women
can acquire sufficient strength of body 'to enable them to earn their own subsistence, the true
definition of independence' (*Works* 5: 155). See Halldenius (2014; 2015: 109–27) and Bergès
(2015: 98–103) on Wollstonecraft's analysis of financial dependence and her plea for an
independence that includes financial self-subsistence.

only in those who are dominated, but also in those who dominate. In *Rights of Woman*, Wollstonecraft famously compares the calamitous effects of the unequal relations between men and women to the moral vices flourishing in standing armies and among the clergy. Concerning the latter, she writes that perhaps 'there cannot be a more forcible contrast than between the servile dependent gait of a poor curate and the courtly mien of a bishop. And the respect and contempt they inspire render the discharge of their separate functions equally useless' (*Works* 5: 86).

Talleyrand-Périgordin, to whom Wollstoncraft dedicated *Rights of Woman*, had recently published a plan for national education in France (Talleyrand-Périgordin 1791). In her dedicatory letter, Wollstonecraft appeals to Talleyrand's republican ideals and compares the situation of slaves and women in order to argue for the latter's education. She writes:

> [T]he more understanding women acquire, the more they will be attached to their duty – comprehending it – for unless they comprehend it, unless their morals be fixed on the same immutable principle as those of man, no authority can make them discharge it in a virtuous manner. They may be convenient slaves, but slavery will have its constant effect, degrading the master and the abject dependent. (*Works* 5: 67–8)

'Liberty is the mother of virtue' (*Works* 5: 105), but can be so only paired with equality and non-arbitrary rule. The unconstrained and arbitrary freedom of action possessed by a tyrant is not liberty in the true sense of the word, since liberty must by definition be based on non-arbitrary lawful rule (*Works* 5: 57; also Halldenius 2015: 101). Depending on social and moral progress or decline, 'woman will be either the friend or slave of man' (*Works* 5: 104). As we saw in Section 5, friendship can only exist among equals (*Works* 5: 10–11). In order to be virtuous, women must have both liberty and equality with other humans, men as well as women.

7.3 The Unity of Virtue

The demand for liberty and equality as a basis for virtue does not in itself imply that virtue must be the *same* for women and men,[39] but Wollstonecraft did also hold the latter view. She emphasizes that 'there is no improving an understanding by halves' (*Works* 5: 249) and that the morals of woman must 'be fixed on the same immutable principle as those of man' (*Works* 5: 67–8). Like Macaulay,

---

[39] Olympe de Gouges is a philosophically interesting counter-example. She demanded liberty and equality for women, but also defended a conception of women's and men's complementary rather than similar virtues. The sexes are supposed to form a 'harmonious togetherness' and 'cooperate in this immortal masterpiece' by being 'intermixed', but without losing their sexed features (Gouges 2011: 30). For a discussion of Gouges' position, see Reuter (2019).

Wollstonecraft develops her argument for universal and gender-neutral virtue as a criticism of Rousseau's account of complementary male and female virtue.[40] In *Emile*, Rousseau rejects the idea of equality based on similarity of the sexes and claims that in 'the union of the sexes each contributes equally to the common aim, but not in the same way' (Rousseau 1979: 358).[41] In order to achieve this goal, argues Rousseau, the education of the two sexes must be guided by two different standards of moral perfectibility. The idea of two different standards for moral development does not in itself create inequality between the sexes, but he continues by introducing a hierarchy between the sexes, which is in stark conflict with his outspoken aim of achieving equality through difference. He claims that 'woman is made specially to please man', for example, and that one sex 'ought to be active and strong, the other passive and weak' (Rousseau 1979: 358; see also Subsection 6.1).

The de facto hierarchy introduced by Rousseau makes him an easy target of Macaulay's and Wollstonecraft's criticisms, and fuels their claims about him as a man of paradoxes (Macaulay 1996: 205; *Letters*: 114). Still, it is important to note that their criticism is not merely targeted at his hierarchical view of the relation between the sexes, but also at the very idea that there can be two separate standards for moral perfectibility. Wollstonecraft presents two inter-related but separate arguments against the idea of gendered virtue. First, she argues, like Macaulay, that morality must be based on immutable principles, which do not allow for differences of sex. Second, she claims, like Price, that virtue constitutes an indivisible whole.

When criticizing Rousseau's model for the education of girls, presented in *Emile* as the education of Emile's future spouse Sophie, Wollstonecraft writes that it is 'the foundation of her character, the principles on which her education was built, that I mean to attack' (*Works* 5: 93). These gendered principles must be abandoned in favour of 'the same immutable principle as those of man' (*Works* 5: 67–8). Virtue has 'only one eternal standard', which knows no difference of sex (*Works* 5: 95). The eternal standard can be known only by reason. Wollstonecraft claims that 'every being may become virtuous by the exercise of its own reason' (*Works* 5: 90) and adds that 'it is a farce to call any being virtuous whose virtues do not result from the exercise of its own reason'

---

[40] For a discussion of Rousseau's position and Wollstonecraft's criticism, see Reuter (2014).

[41] Rousseau is explicitly criticizing the arguments about equality based on similarity developed by authors such as François Poulain de la Barre during the preceding century. Rousseau writes: 'how vain are the disputes as to whether one of the two sexes is superior or whether they are equal – as though each, in fulfilling nature's ends according to its own particular purpose, were thereby less perfect than if it resembled the other more!' (Rousseau 1979: 358); also Reuter (2019).

(*Works* 5: 90). The latter claim is aimed at Rousseau, who held that 'opinion respecting men', but introduced a different standard for women (*Works* 5: 90).

As we saw in Subsection 2.1, Wollstonecraft equates the 'perfectibility of human reason' with the immortality of the human soul (*Work* 5: 122). She argues that those who claim that women 'ought to aim at attaining a very different character' must deny that women have immortal souls (*Works* 5: 88). This is a blasphemous assumption, which no one would like to make. Wollstonecraft uses the doctrine of the immortality of the human soul to claim that 'it should seem, allowing [women] to have souls, that there is but one way appointed by Providence to lead *mankind* to either virtue or happiness' (*Works* 5: 88). Like Price, Wollstonecraft thinks that virtue includes in itself a deontological element. To act virtuously is to act upon immutable moral principles. The deontological aspect of her thought is most visible in *Rights of Men*, where she emphasizes that since the Creator's motive for creating humans must have been wise and good, she is obligated to 'submit to the moral laws which [her] reason deduces from this view of [her] dependence on him' (*Works* 5: 34; see also Subsection 2.3).

In addition to emphasizing the role of immutable principles, Wollstonecraft discusses the role of a virtuous character and the habits needed to acquire such a character. Her account of the unity of virtue is not as explicit as Price's, but we find clear hints in that direction. She claims that women must be allowed to 'acquire human virtues, and by the exercise of their understandings, that stability of character which is the firmest ground to rest our future hopes upon' (*Works* 5: 89). It is thus the understanding that gives a virtuous character its stability, and as we have seen, 'there is no improving an understanding by halves' (*Works* 5: 249; also Subsection 6.1). The necessity to improve the understanding as a whole to achieve a virtuous character culminates in Wollstonecraft's famous rejection of Rousseau's 'wild chimeras'. She writes: 'I still insist ... that women, considered not only as moral, but rational creatures, ought to endeavour to acquire human virtues (or perfections) by the *same* means as men, instead of being educated like a fanciful kind of *half* being – one of Rousseau's wild chimeras' (*Works* 5: 108).

7.4 Mind and Body

The unity of virtue originates in the unity of truth and reason, and the stability of a virtuous character is firmly grounded in the unity of the understanding. Still, acquiring a virtuous character requires habit as well as understanding, and Wollstonecraft perceives understanding in a broader sense than mere reasoning or knowledge. When discussing the goals and practices of education, she writes: '[T]he most perfect education, in my opinion, is such an exercise of the understanding as is best calculated to strengthen the body and form the heart. Or, in other words, to enable the individual to attain such habits of virtue as will render it independent' (*Works* 5: 90). Wollstonecraft posits a strong interrelation between the mind and the body: in order to achieve a strong character, one has to exercise both (*Works* 5: 119). She argues against the fashionable idea that 'men of genius have . . . delicate constitutions', countering 'that strength of mind has, in most cases, been accompanied by superior strength of body' (*Works* 5: 107). Strengthening the body goes hand in hand with forming the heart, and here the formation of a virtuous character relies on the passions as well as reason. It is important to 'let [the heart] expand and feel for all that is human, instead of being narrowed by selfish passions' (*Works* 5: 193). As we saw in Subsection 3.2, Wollstonecraft emphasizes the importance of 'generous feeling', which must be allowed to form a 'permanent character' and fix 'some habit' in order to prevent the development of 'selfish prudence and reason just rising above instinct' (*Works* 5: 181).

The bodily aspect of virtue is essential to Wollstonecraft's discussion of modesty. Her defence of the universal character of virtue culminates in denial of 'the existence of sexual virtues, not excepting modesty' (*Works* 5: 120), and she dedicates a full chapter of *Rights of Woman* to a discussion of the true nature of modesty. Among many of Wollstonecraft's contemporaries, modesty was considered a specifically female virtue, closely connected to chastity, and it was often seen as a character trait rather than a true virtue, derived through the perfection of one's abilities. Wollstonecraft emphasizes that 'modesty is a virtue, not a quality' and as is the case with all virtues, 'those women who have most improved their reason must have the most modesty' (*Works* 5: 192, 193). Modesty is a principal virtue of character and, perceived through the idea of the unity of virtue, the modest person appears as a person in possession of all the virtues, including wisdom and courage as well as generosity (*Works* 5: 191–5).

Wollstonecraft's modesty is also an evident descendant of the originally Aristotelian virtue of *magnanimity* or great-mindedness (*Nicomachean Ethics* IV.3 1123*b*1–2). Like Aristotelian virtue in general, modesty is a mean between extremes. Wollstonecraft points out that modesty is 'equally distant from vanity or presumption' and 'from humility, because humility is a kind of self-abasement' (*Works* 5: 191). Modesty is 'that soberness of mind which teaches a man not to think more highly of himself than he ought to think' though he must at the same time be 'conscious of his own strength' (*Works* 5: 191). As we see from the pronoun in these characterizations, Wollstonecraft counteracts the contemporary femininity of modesty by reminding the reader of its republican and masculine origins. General Washington is her prime example of a modest man. Modesty is masculine in the same sense as the 'grand passions' that exercise and strengthen the understanding (*Works* 5: 179; see Subsections 2.2, 3.1.2 and 3.2). Wollstonecraft contrasts masculinity with feminine weakness, but she does so in order to improve women's education and make women strong and truly modest, not in order to exclude women from the realm of reason and virtue. Education and social circumstances must allow women to strengthen both their minds and bodies in order to develop the true virtue of modesty.

7.5 Aristotelian or Platonist Virtue?

Wollstonecraft's emphasis on modesty as a mean and her accounts of the importance of the passions and habit for acquiring virtue are features of a conception of virtue that is broadly Aristotelian. These features have led some scholars to interpret Wollstonecraft as an Aristotelian virtue ethicist. Natalie Taylor, in particular, has argued that in Aristotle, Wollstonecraft would have found a model where 'the *telos* of human beings is not compromised by generation. Aristotle combines the human and the female sex in a way that forms a whole' (Taylor 2007: 144). Taylor adds that this Aristotelian model would have been a tempting alternative to Rousseau's 'monstrous "half-being"' (Taylor 2007: 144).[42] Taylor correctly points out that Aristotle ties *telos*, or, in Wollstonecraft's terminology, the principle of perfectibility, to the human species and thus emphasizes that it is the same for women and men. Gender differences belong to a metaphysically lesser accidental order.[43] Still, despite a shared *telos*, it is difficult to see that Aristotle's account of virtue would provide Wollstonecraft with a serious alternative to Rousseau's account of gendered virtue. Aristotle does distinguish between male and female virtue and argue that 'the courage and justice of a man and of a woman, are not, as Socrates maintained, the same; the courage of a man is shown in commanding, of a woman in obeying' (*Politics* I 13. 1260*a*21–4).

Taylor's Aristotelian interpretation relies in part on a confusion between Wollstonecraft's notions of virtue and duty. Taylor interprets Wollstonecraft's claim that a woman 'has different duties to fulfil' (*Works* 5: 120) to mean that 'Wollstonecraft, like Aristotle, allows that women may practice different virtues' (Taylor 2007: 161). This is exactly what Wollstonecraft does not allow. She allows for different duties (see Subsection 7.6), but when it comes

---

[42] Natalie Taylor is not claiming that Wollstonecraft had much, if any, direct knowledge of Aristotle's works, but rather that he 'provides a good theoretical grounding for Wollstonecraft's own inquiry into the nature of woman' (Taylor 2007: 116).

[43] On Aristotle's account of gender difference, see Deslauriers (2009).

to virtue, she agrees with the position Aristotle criticizes, which was articulated by the character Socrates in Plato's dialogue *Meno*. Here Socrates gets Meno to admit that the same virtue of justice makes men and women rule well, despite the practical fact that men rule in the state and women rule in the household (*Meno* 73a–b). As we saw in Subsection 7.4, Wollstonecraft argues that even modesty, which her contemporaries characterized as a female virtue, is the same for women and men. Likewise, justice, courage and generosity are the same virtues regardless of whether they belong to a woman or a man. Wollstonecraft disagrees with both Rousseau's view that women and men should develop different and complementary virtues and Aristotle's view that a particular virtue such as justice or courage takes a different form in women, who ought to obey, and men, who ought to command.

Wollstonecraft's emphasis on the passions and imagination (see Subsection 4.1) indicates a departure from Price's Platonist rationalism. She is also more detailed than Price in her discussions of habituation and, in particular, education. Sandrine Bergès has interpreted Wollstonecraft's emphasis on these features of virtue as a form of Aristotelian virtue ethics (Bergès 2013: 65–85). Some topics of Aristotelian origin, such as the virtue of magnanimity and the idea of virtue friendship (see Subsection 5.1), were deeply immersed in Wollstonecraft's philosophical context and indeed appear in her writings in a form that can be identified as Aristotelian. Other aspects, such as the role of the passions in the habituation of virtue, were given various forms by authors from Shaftesbury to Rousseau and Adam Smith. These influences reached Wollstonecraft as part of a contemporary discussion of the roles of the passions, moral sentiments and moral sense, and it is much more difficult to trace in them a characteristically Aristotelian core. Concerning the relations between reason, passion and imagination, and their respective roles in the acquisition of virtue, I am more inclined to emphasize the originality of Wollstonecraft's thought than to call her an Aristotelian virtue ethicist.

Price repeatedly refers to Plato's writings, but Aristotle is less present in authors that we know Wollstonecraft read. Whereas she refers to Plato as 'a great philosopher' (*Works* 5: 23), we find no corresponding admiration of Aristotle. As Bergès noted, the absence of Aristotle from Wollstonecraft's intellectual horizon may well in part be due to the fact that Aristotelianism was strongly associated with Catholicism and not well regarded in eighteenth-century England (Bergès 2013: 67). To conclude this subsection, we should address the question posed in the subtitle: did Wollstonecraft hold a Platonist or Aristotelian conception of virtue? I think there are several answers. First, if we restrict the use of the terms Platonism or Aristotelianism to explicit instances such as Price's explicitly Platonist concept of virtue, then Wollstonecraft's understanding of virtue was neither Platonist nor Aristotelian. Second, if we look for Platonist and Aristotelian topics in Wollstonecraft's discussions of virtue, I do think we find both. Third, if we look specifically at Wollstonecraft's criticism of gendered virtue and her conception of the ungendered nature of virtue, her conception is in an important respect Platonist, relying on the same form of argument as Plato's discussion in *Meno* (73a–b).

7.6 Human Duties

Following the republican tradition, Wollstonecraft distinguishes between moral and civic duties. When discussing women's duties in *Rights of Woman*, Wollstonecraft begins by emphasizing that 'without rights there cannot be any incumbent duties' (*Works* 5: 215). If a woman is to 'discharge her civil duties', she must individually have 'the protection of civil laws' (*Works* 5: 216). As we saw in Subsection 7.2, virtue requires liberty. Similarly, duties become binding only when legal rights secure the independence of the being who is supposed to discharge those duties. Importantly, humans do not have duties only towards others, but also towards themselves. The latter are specifically moral duties. Wollstonecraft writes: 'The being who discharges the duties of its station is independent; and, speaking of women at large, their first duty is to themselves as rational creatures, and the next, in point of importance, as citizens, is that, which includes so many, of a mother' (*Works* 5: 216).

Wollstonecraft argues, once again, that in order to be good mothers, women must be able to exercise their reason freely. A rational creature's first duty is to herself as a rational being. Only when independence has secured the fulfilment of this duty can she fulfil other duties, including the duty of motherhood. Here Wollstonecraft describes the duties of a mother as civil duties, but she also claims that 'the care of children in their infancy is one of the grand duties annexed to the female character by nature' (*Works* 5: 222). When referring to motherhood as a duty annexed by nature, she seems to think of one specific duty related to motherhood, the duty to breastfeed one's children rather than send them to a wet nurse (*Works* 5: 220, 223; see also Bergès 2016). There are natural circumstances which differentiate what is implied by the duties of motherhood and fatherhood, but for both parents these are in themselves civic duties. Wollstonecraft emphasizes that she treats 'of the peculiar duties of women' as she 'should treat of the peculiar duties of a citizen or father' (*Works* 5: 132). The duties of mothers and fathers are also interdependent. Wollstonecraft concludes that when women become 'rational creatures, and free citizens, ... they will quickly become good wives, and mothers; that is – if men do not neglect the duties of husbands and fathers' (*Works* 5: 250).

The discharge of duties depends on the exercise of one's reason and on independence that is not only moral and social, but political. When Wollstonecraft denies the existence of 'sexual virtues', she adds: 'Women, I allow, may have different duties to fulfil; but they are *human* duties, and the principles that should regulate the discharge of them, I sturdily maintain, must be the same' (*Works* 5: 120). The discharge of human duties must be regulated by the same immutable principles, which belong to virtue. In other words, duties may vary, but principles and virtues remain the same. We can again compare Wollstonecraft's position to Plato's argument in *Meno* (73a–b): women's duties belong to the household and men's duties to the state, but their virtues remain the same. From an emancipatory point of view, it may seem disappointing that Wollstonecraft, like Plato, allows the majority of women to discharge most of their duties in the household, but it is crucial to note that neither of them are here describing a necessary social order grounded on human nature. On the contrary, since Wollstonecraft and Plato think that women and men share the same essentials of human nature and the same virtues, we can imagine societies where the sexes discharge the same duties.[44]

Wollstonecraft argues that the majority of women should not 'be taken out of their families', but immediately adds that the same is true for the majority of men (*Works* 5: 132–3). She emphasizes that the 'more reasonably organized' a society is, the less it needs 'heroic virtues', that is, exertions on the battlefield or during periods of political unrest (*Works* 5: 133). Neither does she think that the group of people that devote their lives to public activities should be exclusively male. Like her fellow radicals, Wollstonecraft was critical of the British system of political representation based on landownership. She writes: '[A]s the whole system of representation is now, in this country, only a convenient handle for despotism, [women] need not complain, for they are as well represented as a numerous class of hard working mechanics, who pay for the support of royalty when they can scarcely stop their children's mouths with bread' (*Works* 5: 217).

---

[44] For Plato's account, see *Republic* V 449a–468a. My point is not that we should consider Plato a feminist or even a forerunner of feminism. He was not, if a demand for the emancipation of women is a necessary condition for calling an argument feminist. Still, feminists used his arguments widely and he was referred to as one of the great defenders of women as late as Harriet Taylor Mill's *Enfranchisement of Women* (1851); see Taylor Mill (1983: 11).

A system in which hard work or even taxpaying do not secure parliamentary representation is unfair and needs to be profoundly reformed. The reform must give not only hard-working mechanics, but also women the possibility to represent themselves. Aware that her remark may 'excite laughter', Wollstonecraft writes that she really thinks 'women ought to have representatives, instead of being arbitrarily governed without having any direct share allowed them in the deliberation of government' (*Works* 5: 217). As Lena Halldenius argues, Wollstonecraft grounds her views on political representation in a critical reinterpretation of republican ideas. Wollstonecraft criticizes the republican idea of a symbolic people that can be represented by idealized wise statesmen, but relies on republican ideas of freedom and duty in her criticism (Halldenius 2016: 179–82). Political societies are not ideal, so interest groups must represent themselves to have political freedom. Women are arbitrarily governed, as Wollstonecraft writes, if they cannot freely participate in the deliberations of government, including the passing of the laws they are required to obey.

To participate in politics, women need to be educated; Wollstonecraft discusses both general education that gives everybody the opportunity to exercise their minds and education for the professions. 'Women might certainly study the art of healing, and be physicians as well as nurses', she writes, and they 'might, also, study politics, and settle their benevolence on the broadest basis' (*Works* 5: 218). If women were 'educated in a more orderly manner' they might likewise pursue businesses 'of various kinds' (*Works* 5: 218). Financial independence saves women from 'common and legal prostitution', when they are not forced to marry for support (*Works* 5: 218). Women need financial independence to 'have a civil existence in the state, married or single' and so that 'their private virtue' can become 'a public benefit' (*Works* 5: 219). When educated to be morally as well as financially independent, women become virtuous, able to shape their destinies and free.

8 Conclusions

Wollstonecraft places the question of gender at the core of her moral philosophy. We have seen that her interest in the liberation of women goes hand in hand with her interest in true virtue. One cannot be achieved without the other. It is important to grasp the necessity of this dependence. Wollstonecraft's two major goals – true virtue and the liberation of women – are both values in themselves. Neither has a mere instrumental value. The right kind of education is a necessary condition for liberation as well as virtue, and again it would be a mistake to see education as instrumental. Rather, education is a necessary aspect of liberty and virtue. Education is, according to Wollstonecraft, to be 'the first step to form a being advancing gradually towards perfection' (*Works* 5: 122).

Wollstonecraft's systematic inclusion of gender is in itself unique in the history of moral philosophy. Rousseau made a similar attempt, but as Wollstonecraft demonstrates, he fails to give a coherent account. Rousseau purported to combine equality and gender difference, but he ended up claiming that 'woman is made specially to please man' (Rousseau 1979: 358). The problem with Rousseau's account is not merely his derogatory view of women, but the paradoxes he ends up accepting. Wollstonecraft learned from his philosophy of education and from his emphasis on thinking for oneself. She is often reading Rousseau against himself, as when she states that both sexes can become virtuous only by exercising their own reason (*Works* 5: 90). Wollstonecraft pinpoints how Rousseau compromises the consistency of his moral system when he makes virtue dependent on the ability to think for oneself while simultaneously making the pleasure of men the goal of women's moral behaviour. Wollstonecraft shows that Rousseau's failure follows from the necessary connection that she draws between the liberation of women and true virtue.

Wollstonecraft is still missing from most general accounts of the history of moral philosophy. J. B. Schneewind's influential *The Invention of Autonomy* (1998) is a good example. He paints a detailed, broad and learned picture of how the idea of self-governance culminates in Kant's idea of autonomy. Schneewind gives many previously neglected authors due attention, but does not mention any female thinkers. The exclusion of women goes hand in hand with the exclusion of the gender question. Schneewind discusses Rousseau's emphasis on the ability to think for oneself and its influence on Kant in some detail, but he makes his discussion explicitly gender-neutral by referring to 'people' rather than men (Schneewind 1998: 488). Schneewind wants to modernize Rousseau by dismissing his views on women, but because he excludes the gendered nature of Rousseau's views he finds no need to discuss Wollstonecraft's detailed criticism of Rousseau (see also Reuter 2018).

The exclusion of Wollstonecraft from the canon of moral philosophy has consequences far beyond the question of gender. She belongs to a tradition of moral philosophy according to which morality is based on reason, but she pays more attention to the passions and the imagination than do her fellow intellectualists, including Richard Price and Catharine Macaulay. Wollstonecraft's combined interest in the strengths of reason and imagination is unique. She follows Rousseau in thinking that the imagination gives birth to new passions, but due to her greater optimism about the strength of reason, she emphasizes the benevolent possibilities of these passions rather than their malevolent threats.

Price is himself too often neglected as a moral philosopher. A parallel reading of his and Wollstonecraft's thought on virtue draws our attention to two points of particular interest. First, Price emphasizes that virtue is in itself obligating (see Subsection 7.1). This view is still relevant to our twenty-first-century discussions of the relations between virtue ethics and post-Kantian forms of deontological ethics. Second, Price's explicit attempt to combine the unity of virtue with 'an endless variety of cases' (Price 1758: 286) is likewise deeply relevant to much later discussion of prima facie ethics. Wollstonecraft inserts both features in her conception of the necessary relation between true virtue and women's liberation. Women must be free so that they can be obligated to think for themselves, and they must think for themselves in order to act virtuously under changing circumstances.

Finally, Wollstonecraft's moral philosophy has a practical orientation. We have seen that her moral thought is founded in metaphysics, which is inter-twined with her theological views. She was evidently aware of metaphysical debates, for instance on free will and innate knowledge, but she was also aware that these are questions that 'metaphysicians have not yet brought to an issue' (*Works* 7: 321; see Subsections 2.2 and 6.2). Instead of engaging in these metaphysical disputes, Wollstonecraft sought common ground. She was a deeply undogmatic thinker, a religious critic of all religious denominations (Godwin 1987: 272). She was more interested in the achievement of virtue than in metaphysical theories.

We can (with some limitations) read Wollstonecraft's works as part of a late eighteenth-century post-metaphysical turn, but she was neither a transcendental nor a utilitarian thinker. Wollstonecraft stops short of Kant's conception of moral agents as autonomous self-legislating beings (see Subsection 2.3). Concerning emerging utilitarian ideas, she agrees with Macaulay, who rejects the idea that morality can be based on the mutable concept of utility as defined by human beings (see Subsection 7.1). The problem is not utility as such, but both authors hold that utility must ultimately be based on divine truth, not on human sentiments and desires. According to Wollstonecraft, if truth is sacri-ficed, 'virtue becomes a relative idea, having no other foundation than utility [of which] men pretend arbitrarily to judge, shaping it to their own convenience' (*Works* 5: 120). Again, we see how Wollstonecraft's plea for the liberty of women converges with her conception of true virtue.

Abbreviations

Works 1–7   Wollstonecraft, M. (1989). *The Works of Mary Wollstonecraft*, 7 vols., eds. J. Todd & M. Butler with E. Rees-Mogg. London: William Pickering.

Letters   Wollstonecraft, M. (2003). *The Collected Letters of Mary Wollstonecraft*, ed. J. Todd. London: Penguin Books.

Appendix

A Brief Chronology of Mary Wollstonecraft's Life and Works

1759	Mary Wollstonecraft (MW) is born on 27 April in Spitalfields, London, as the second of Edward John Wollstonecraft (EJW) and Elizabeth Dickson Wollstonecraft's seven children.
1763–77	The Wollstonecraft family lives an unstable life at various locations in the London area, in Yorkshire and in Wales, as EJW's finances are deteriorating due to his failed attempts to set himself up as a gentleman farmer and to other unsuccessful enterprises.
1778	MW leaves her family home, now set up in Walworth, London, in order to take up employment as a ladies' companion in Bath.
1781–3	MW moves back to her family home in order to nurse her mother, who dies in 1782. MW cares for her younger siblings as well as for her friend Fanny Blood's family.
1784	With her sister Eliza and Fanny Blood, MW sets up a school for girls at Newington Green, a vicinity known for its large population of rational dissenters. MW meets Richard Price, who is living in the area.
1785	Fanny Blood marries and moves to Lisbon. MW visits her in order to assist her during her pregnancy and childbirth. Fanny and the baby both die. The journey to Lisbon inspires MW's first novel *Mary: A Fiction* (1788).
1786	Having returned to London, MW closes the school at Newington Green because of financial problems. She takes employment as a governess for the Kingsborough family in Ireland.
1787	MW's first book, *Thoughts on the Education of Daughters*, is published by Joseph Johnson. During this time, MW reads Jean-Jacques Rousseau's *Emile* (1762). She is dismissed by Lady Kingsborough and returns to London, where she starts working as a reader and translator for Joseph Johnson and becomes acquainted with radicals such as Thomas Holcroft and Henry Fuseli.
1788	MW publishes *Mary: A Fiction; Original Stories from Real Life*; and a translation of Jacques Necker's book titled *Of the Importance of Religious Opinions*. She begins to review books for Joseph Johnson's periodical the *Analytical Review*.

1789   *The Female Reader* is published under the pseudonym Mr Cresswick.

1790   MW publishes two more translations and *A Vindication of the Rights of Men* as a defence against Edmund Burke's attack on Richard Price and the French Revolution. She reviews Catharine Macaulay's *Letters on Education* for the *Analytical Review.*

1791   MW publishes a second edition of *Original Stories*, with illustrations by William Blake.

1792   MW publishes *A Vindication of the Rights of Woman* and moves to Paris, where she meets other English expatriates such as Helen Maria Williams and Thomas Paine.

1793   In Paris, MW meets the American radical and entrepreneur Gilbert Imlay, with whom she has a love affair. France declares war on England and MW is registered as Imlay's wife, though she is not married to him, to provide her the protection of American citizenship.

1794   MW moves to Le Havre, where her daughter Fanny Imlay is born. *An Historical and Moral View of the Origin and Progress of the French Revolution* is published in London.

1795   MW returns to London and attempts suicide after discovering Imlay's affair with another woman. During the summer, she travels to Sweden, Norway and Denmark in an attempt to trace a missing shipment that Imlay has attempted to transport through the embargo between France and England. Upon her return to London, she attempts suicide for a second time.

1796   *Letters Written During a Short Residence in Sweden, Norway, and Denmark* is published. MW begins her love relationship with William Godwin.

1797   MW and Godwin marry in March. Their daughter Mary (Wollstonecraft Godwin, married Shelley) is born on 30 August. MW dies from complications following childbirth on 10 September.

1798   Godwin edits and publishes MW's four-volume *Posthumous Works*, which includes, for example, the unfinished novel *The Wrongs of Woman, or Maria*; her *Letters to Imlay*; *Letter on the Present Character of the French Nation*; and *Hints*. Godwin also publishes *Memoirs of the Author of A Vindication of the Rights of Woman.*

References

Abbey, R. (1999). Back to the Future: Marriage as Friendship in the Thought of Mary Wollstonecraft. *Hypatia: A Journal of Feminist Philosophy* 14(3), 78–95.

Aristotle (1984a). *Nicomachean Ethics*, trans. W. D. Ross, rev. J. O. Urmson. In J. Barnes, ed., *The Complete Works of Aristotle*, vol. 2. Princeton, NJ: Princeton University Press, pp. 1729–1867.

Aristotle (1984b). *Politics*, trans. B. Jowett. In J. Barnes, ed., *The Complete Works of Aristotle*, vol. 2. Princeton, NJ: Princeton University Press, pp. 1986–2129.

Bergès, S. (2013). *The Routledge Guidebook to Wollstonecraft's* A Vindication of the Rights of Woman. London: Routledge.

Bergès, S. (2015). *A Feminist Perspective on Virtue Ethics*. Basingstoke: Palgrave Macmillan.

Bergès, S. (2016). Wet-Nursing and Political Participation: The Republican Approaches to Motherhood of Mary Wollstonecraft and Sophie de Grouchy. In S. Bergès and A. Coffee, eds., *The Social and Political Philosophy of Mary Wollstonecraft*. Oxford: Oxford University Press, pp. 201–17.

Bergès, S. and A. Coffee (2016). Introduction. In S. Bergès and A. Coffee, eds., *The Social and Political Philosophy of Mary Wollstonecraft*. Oxford: Oxford University Press, pp. 1–13.

Botting, E. H. (2016). Mary Wollstonecraft, Children's Human Rights, and Animal Ethics. In S. Bergès and A. Coffee, eds., *The Social and Political Philosophy of Mary Wollstonecraft*. Oxford: Oxford University Press, pp. 92–116.

Bour, I. (2019). Epistemology. In S. Bergès, E. H. Botting and A. Coffee, eds., *The Wollstonecraftian Mind*. London: Routledge, pp. 311–22.

Coffee, A. (2013). Mary Wollstonecraft, Freedom and the Enduring Power of Social Domination. *European Journal of Political Theory* 12(2), 116–35.

Coffee, A. (2014). Freedom as Independence: Mary Wollstonecraft and the Grand Blessing of Life. *Hypatia: A Journal of Feminist Philosophy* 29(4), 908–24.

Coffee, A. (2016). Mary Wollstonecraft, Public Reason, and the Virtuous Republic. In S. Bergès and A. Coffee, eds., *The Social and Political Philosophy of Mary Wollstonecraft*. Oxford: Oxford University Press, pp. 182–200.

Deslauriers, M. (2009). Sexual Difference in Aristotle's *Politics* and His Biology. *Classical World* 102(3), 215–31.

Dumler-Winckler, E. (2019). Theology and Religion. In S. Bergès, E. H. Botting and A. Coffee, eds., *The Wollstonecraftian Mind*. London: Routledge, pp. 297–310.

Frazer, E. (2008). Mary Wollstonecraft on Politics and Friendship. *Political Studies* 56, 237–56.

Gatens, M. (1991). 'The Oppressed State of My Sex': Wollstonecraft on Reason, Feeling and Equality. In M. L. Shanley and C. Pateman, eds., *Feminist Interpretations and Political Theory*. Cambridge: Polity Press, pp. 112–28.

Godwin, W. (1987). Memoirs of the Author of 'The Rights of Woman'. In M. Wollstonecraft and W. Godwin, *A Short Residence in Sweden, Norway and Denmark and Memoirs of the Author of 'Rights of Woman'*, ed. R. Holmes. London: Penguin Books, pp. 204–73.

Goldman, E. (1981). Mary Wollstonecraft, Her Tragic Life and Her Passionate Struggle for Freedom. *Feminist Studies* 7(1), 114–21.

Gouges, O. de (2011). The Rights of Woman. To the Queen. In J. Cole, ed., *Between the Queen and the Cabby: Olympe de Gouges's Rights of Woman*. Montreal: McGill-Queen's University Press, pp. 28–41.

Green, K. (1997). The Passions and the Imagination in Wollstonecraft's Theory of Moral Judgement. *Utilitas* 9(3), 271–90.

Green, K. (2019). Book Review of Sandrine Bergès and Alan Coffee, eds., *The Social and Political Philosophy of Mary Wollstonecraft*. Mind Association Occasional Series. Oxford: Oxford University Press, 2016. *Philosophical Review* 128(2), 228–32.

Green, K. (2020). *Catharine Macaulay's Republican Enlightenment*. New York: Routledge.

Greenberg, S. (2013). Liberty and Necessity. In J. A. Harris, ed., *The Oxford Handbook of British Philosophy in the Eighteenth Century*. Oxford: Oxford University Press, pp. 248–69.

Gunther-Canada, W. (2001). *Rebel Writer: Mary Wollstonecraft and Enlightenment Politics*. DeKalb: Northern Illinois University Press.

Gunther-Canada, W. (2003). Cultivating Virtue: Catharine Macaulay and Mary Wollstonecraft on Civic Education. *Women and Politics* 25(3), 47–70.

Guyer, P. (2013). The Pleasures of the Imagination and the Objects of Taste. In J. A. Harris, ed., *The Oxford Handbook of British Philosophy in the Eighteenth Century*. Oxford: Oxford University Press, pp. 393–429.

Halldenius, L. (2007). The Primacy of Right: On the Triad of Liberty, Equality and Virtue in Wollstonecraft's Political Thought. *British Journal for the History of Philosophy* 15(1), 75–99.

Halldenius, L. (2014). Mary Wollstonecraft's Feminist Critique of Property: On Becoming a Thief from Principle. *Hypatia: A Journal of Feminist Philosophy* 29(4), 942–57.

Halldenius, L. (2015). *Mary Wollstonecraft and Feminist Republicanism: Independence, Rights and Experience of Unfreedom*. London: Pickering & Chatto.

Halldenius, L. (2016). Representation in Mary Wollstonecraft's Political Philosophy. In S. Bergès and A. Coffee, eds., *The Social and Political Philosophy of Mary Wollstonecraft*. Oxford: Oxford University Press, pp. 166–82.

Harris, J. A. (2005). *Of Liberty and Necessity: The Free Will Debate in Eighteenth-Century British Philosophy*. Oxford: Oxford University Press.

Harris, J. A. (2013). The Government of the Passions. In J. A. Harris, ed., *The Oxford Handbook of British Philosophy in the Eighteenth Century*. Oxford: Oxford University Press, pp. 270–88.

Helm, B. (2021). Love. In E. N. Zalta, ed., *Stanford Encyclopedia of Philosophy*, fall 2021 edition. https://plato.stanford.edu/archives/fall2021/entries/love.

Hickman, L. (2019). Mixing Politics with the Pulpit: Eternal Immutable Morality and Richard Price's Political Radicalism. In D. Hedley and D. Leech, eds., *Revisioning Cambridge Platonism: Sources and Legacy*. Cham: Springer, pp. 159–73.

Hutton, S. (2007). Virtue, God and Stoicism in the Thought of Elizabeth Carter and Catharine Macaulay. In J. Broad and K. Green, eds., *Virtue, Liberty, and Toleration: Political Ideas of European Women, 1400–1800*. Dordrecht: Springer, pp. 137–48.

Hutton, S. (2021). Radicalism, Religion and Mary Wollstonecraft. *Intellectual History Review* 31(1), 181–98.

Kaplan, C. (1986). *Sea Changes: Essays on Culture and Feminism*. London: Verso.

Kendrick, N. (2016). Wollstonecraft on Marriage as Virtue Friendship. In S. Bergès and A. Coffee, eds., *The Social and Political Philosophy of Mary Wollstonecraft*. Oxford: Oxford University Press, pp. 34–49.

Kendrick, N. (2019). Marriage, Love, and Friendship. In S. Bergès, E. H. Botting and A. Coffee, eds., *The Wollstonecraftian Mind*. London: Routledge, pp. 381–90.

Khin Zaw, S. (1998). The Reasonable Heart: Mary Wollstonecraft's View of the Relation between Reason and Feeling in Morality, Moral Psychology, and Moral Development. *Hypatia: A Journal of Feminist Philosophy* 13(1), 78–117.

Kivy, P. (2013). Genius and the Creative Imagination. In J. A. Harris, ed., *The Oxford Handbook of British Philosophy in the Eighteenth Century*. Oxford: Oxford University Press, pp. 468–87.

Locke, J. (1964). Some Thoughts Concerning Education. In P. Grey, ed., *John Locke on Education*. New York: Teachers College Press, pp. 19–176.

Locke, J. (1975). *An Essay Concerning Human Understanding*, ed. P. H. Nidditch. Oxford: Oxford University Press.

Macaulay, C. (1996). *Letters on Education*. Facsimile of the 1790 edition. London: William Pickering.

Macaulay Graham, C. (1783). *A Treatise on the Immutability of Moral Truth*. London: A. Hamilton.

Mackenzie, C. (1993). Reason and Sensibility: The Ideal of Women's Self-Governance in the Writings of Mary Wollstonecraft. *Hypatia: A Journal of Feminist Philosophy* 8(4), 181–203.

O'Brien, K. (2009). *Women and Enlightenment in Eighteenth-Century Britain*. Cambridge: Cambridge University Press.

Perinetti, D. (2013). The Nature of Virtue. In J. A. Harris, ed., *The Oxford Handbook of British Philosophy in the Eighteenth Century*. Oxford: Oxford University Press, pp. 333–68.

Plato (1767). *The Banquet, a Dialogue of Plato Concerning Love: The Second Part*, trans. F. Sydenham. London: W. Sandby.

Plato (1777). *Phedon: or, a Dialogue of the Immortality of the Soul: From Plato the Divine Philosopher*, trans. anonymous. London: J. Davidson.

Plato (1993). *The Symposium*, ed. and trans. W. S. Cobb. In *The Symposium and the Phaedrus: Plato's Erotic Dialogues*. Albany: State University of New York Press, pp. 15–59.

Plato (1998). *Republic*, ed. and trans. R. Waterfield. Oxford: Oxford University Press.

Plato (2005). *Meno*, ed. and trans. R. Waterfield. In *Meno and Other Dialogues: Charmides, Laches, Lysis, Meno*. Oxford: Oxford University Press, pp. 97–143.

Plato (2008). *Laws* 10, ed. and trans. R. Mayhew. Oxford: Oxford University Press.

Price, R. (1758). *A Review of the Principal Questions and Difficulties in Morals; Particularly Those Relating to the Original of Our Ideas of Virtue, Its Nature, Foundation, Reference to the Deity, Obligation, Subject-Matter, and Sanctions*. London: A. Millar.

Price, R. (1767). *Four Dissertations*. London: A. Millar & T. Cadell.

Price, R. (1991). *Political Writings*, ed. D. O. Thomas. Cambridge: Cambridge University Press.

Reuter, M. (2005). Mary Wollstonecraft on Love and Friendship. In Å. Carlson, ed., *Philosophical Aspects on Emotions*. Stockholm: Thales, pp. 119–39.

Reuter, M. (2007). Catharine Macaulay and Mary Wollstonecraft on the Will. In J. Broad and K. Green, eds., *Virtue, Liberty, and Toleration: Political Ideas of European Women, 1400–1800*. Dordrecht: Springer, pp. 149–69.

Reuter, M. (2010). Revolution, Virtue and Duty: Aspects of Politics, Religion and Morality in Mary Wollstonecraft's Thought. In M. T. Mjaaland, O. Sigurdson and S. Thorgeirsdottir, eds., *The Body Unbound: Philosophical Perspectives on Politics, Embodiment and Religion*. Newcastle upon Tyne: Cambridge Scholars Publishing, pp. 107–22.

Reuter, M. (2014). 'Like a Fanciful Kind of *Half* Being': Mary Wollstonecraft's Criticism of Jean-Jacques Rousseau. *Hypatia: A Journal of Feminist Philosophy* 29(4), 925–41.

Reuter, M. (2016). The Role of the Passions in Mary Wollstonecraft's Notion of Virtue. In S. Bergès and A. Coffee, eds., *The Social and Political Philosophy of Mary Wollstonecraft*. Oxford: Oxford University Press, pp. 50–66.

Reuter, M. (2017). Jean-Jacques Rousseau and Mary Wollstonecraft on the Imagination. *British Journal for the History of Philosophy* 25(6), 1116–36.

Reuter, M. (2018). Mary Wollstonecraft's Contribution to the 'Invention of Autonomy'. In S. Bergès and A. L. Siani, eds., *Women Philosophers on Autonomy: Historical and Contemporary Perspectives*. New York: Routledge, pp. 112–30.

Reuter, M. (2019). Equality and Difference in Olympe de Gouges' *Les droits de la femme: A La Reine*. *Australasian Philosophical Review* 3(4), 422–31.

Rousseau, J-J. (1763). *Emilius and Sophia: or, a New System of Education. Translated from the French of Mr. J. J. Rousseau, Citizen of Geneva. By the Translator of Eloisa*, trans. W. Kenrick, vol. 4. London: T. Becket & P. A. de Hondt.

Rousseau, J-J. (1979). *Emile or On Education*, trans. A. Bloom. New York: Basic Books.

Rousseau, J-J. (2002). *The Social Contract and The First and Second Discourses*, trans. and ed. S. Dunn. New Haven, CT: Yale University Press.

Sapiro, V. (1992). *A Vindication of Political Virtue: The Political Theory of Mary Wollstonecraft*. Chicago: University of Chicago Press.

Schmitter, A. M. (2013). Passions, Affections, Sentiments: Taxonomy and Terminology. In J. A. Harris, ed., *The Oxford Handbook of British Philosophy in the Eighteenth Century*. Oxford: Oxford University Press, pp. 197–225.

Schneewind, J. B. (1998). *The Invention of Autonomy: A History of Modern Moral Philosophy*. Cambridge: Cambridge University Press.

Smith, A. (2002). *The Theory of Moral Sentiments*, ed. K. Haakonssen. Cambridge: Cambridge University Press.

Smith, O. (2019). Rational Dissent. In S. Bergès, E.H. Botting, and A. Coffee, eds., *The Wollstonecraftian Mind*. London: Routledge, pp. 49–62.

Spencer, J. (2012). 'The Link Which Unites Man with Brutes': Enlightenment Feminism, Women and Animals. *Intellectual History Review* 22(3), 427–44.

Stanton, T. (2013). Locke and His Influence. In J. A. Harris, ed., *The Oxford Handbook of British Philosophy in the Eighteenth Century*. Oxford: Oxford University Press, pp. 21–40.

Swift, J. (2005). *Gulliver's Travels*, eds. C. Rawson and I. Higgins. Oxford: Oxford University Press.

Talleyrand-Périgordin, C. M. de (1791). *Rapport sur l'instruction publique*. Paris: Baudouin & Du Point.

Taylor, B. (2003). *Mary Wollstonecraft and the Feminist Imagination*. Cambridge: Cambridge University Press.

Taylor, N. F. (2007). *The Rights of Woman as Chimera: The Political Philosophy of Mary Wollstonecraft*. New York: Routledge.

Taylor Mill, H. (1983). Enfranchisement of Women. In John Stuart Mill and Harriet Taylor Mill, *The Subjection of Women & Enfranchisement of Women*. London: Virago, pp. 1–43.

Todd, J. (2000). *Mary Wollstonecraft: A Revolutionary Life*. London: Weidenfeld & Nicolson.

Tomaselli, S. (2019). 'Have Ye Not Heard That We Cannot Serve Two Masters?': The Platonism of Mary Wollstonecraft. In D. Hedley and D. Leech, eds., *Revisioning Cambridge Platonism: Sources and Legacy*. Cham: Springer, pp. 175–89.

Tomaselli, S. (2021). *Wollstonecraft: Philosophy, Passion, and Politics*. Princeton, NJ: Princeton University Press.

Vernon, R. (2005). *Friends, Citizens, Strangers: Essays on Where We Belong*. Toronto: University of Toronto Press.

Whale, J. (2000). *Imagination under Pressure, 1789–1832*. Cambridge: Cambridge University Press.

Woolf, V. (1989). *A Room of One's Own*. San Diego, CA: Harvest.

Woolf, V. (2001). Mary Wollstonecraft. In *On Women and Writing: Her Essays, Assessments and Arguments*, ed. M. Barrett. London: The Women's Press.

Acknowledgements

Since 2012, I have been part of an informal group of Wollstonecraft scholars including Sandrine Bergès, Alan Coffee and Lena Halldenius. Their work and our joint discussions have had a great impact on my ways of understanding Wollstonecraft's works. I would like to thank them for their uplifting academic comradeship. Outside this group, I have had the benefit of ongoing philosophical discussions with Marguerite Deslauriers and Tuomas Parsio. Jacqueline Broad, Frans Svensson, Kate Sotejeff-Wilson and two anonymous referees have made excellent revisions and suggestions. My profound additional gratitude goes to family, friends and horses, who have provided support as well as distraction.

Cambridge Elements ≡

Women in the History of Philosophy

Jacqueline Broad
Monash University

Jacqueline Broad is Associate Professor of Philosophy at Monash University, Australia. Her area of expertise is early modern philosophy, with a special focus on seventeenth- and eighteenth-century women philosophers. She is the author of *Women Philosophers of the Seventeenth Century* (Cambridge University Press, 2002), *A History of Women's Political Thought in Europe, 1400–1700* (with Karen Green; Cambridge University Press, 2009), and *The Philosophy of Mary Astell: An Early Modern Theory of Virtue* (Oxford University Press, 2015).

Advisory Board

Dirk Baltzly, *University of Tasmania*
Sandrine Bergès, *Bilkent University*
Marguerite Deslauriers, *McGill University*
Karen Green, *University of Melbourne*
Lisa Shapiro, *Simon Fraser University*
Emily Thomas, *Durham University*

About the Series

In this Cambridge Elements series, distinguished authors provide concise and structured introductions to a comprehensive range of prominent and lesser-known figures in the history of women's philosophical endeavour, from ancient times to the present day.

Cambridge Elements ☰

Women in the History of Philosophy

Elements in the Series

A full series listing is available at: www.cambridge.org/EWHP

Printed in the United States
by Baker & Taylor Publisher Services